THE LAZY GARDENER

Letting the Garden Grow by Itself

D1732661

A path and a gate become inviting when bordered by tall white hybrid lilium *and some low-growing perennials.*

THE LAZY GARDENER

Letting the Garden Grow by Itself

Ruth King

Illustrated By Anita Hart

Drake Publishers Inc   New York • London

To . . .

Amos Pettingill whose informative book and catalogues convinced me to try gardening.

Anita Hart who convinced me to try writing and also illustrated this book.

Edward, Debbie, Judy, Jonny and Gideon who convinced me to try both.

Published in 1977 by
Drake Publishers, Inc.
801 Second Avenue
New York, N.Y. 10017

FEB 21 '78

Library of Congress Cataloging in Publication Data

King, Ruth S
      The lazy gardener.

      1. Perennials. 2. Flower gardening. I. Hart,
Anita, joint author. II. Title.
SB434.K56   635.9'32   76-55429
ISBN 0-8473-1514-2

Book Design: Harold Franklin
Art Direction: A. A. Horowitz

Printed in the United States of America

contents

ACKNOWLEDGMENTS

I am very grateful to the staffs of Hollandia Gardens in Bethel, White Flower Farm in Litchfield, and Lexington Gardens in Newtown, for their advice and courtesy. I am also indebted to Wayside Gardens in Hodges, South Carolina, the source of some of my favorite perennials, for the lovely photographs they shared with me. Mr. Joseph Mayo of Cheshire, Connecticut was incredibly prompt in forwarding pictures from White Flower Farm and equally patient waiting for their return. Joan Lee Faust, author and editor of the garden section of the New York Times, gave me sound advice and encouragement. The Image Bank and Berkey Photolabs were very helpful in locating photographs for me. Doris Schleisner spent hours tracking down the lovely pictures, and Nick and Mary De Thill generously allowed me to use their collection of catalogues and magazines. Jay Willie helped with garden chores, while the Salomons, Ruth Diamond, and Robin Kyriakis pushed me to the typewriter. Many thanks are also due to the cordial staff of Drake, most especially to Ted Gottfried.

PREFACE

T.S. Eliot said, "April is the cruelest month." Well, maybe for poets it is, but for those of us in northern climates, it's a lovely month. After spending the winter with runny noses and rheumy eyes, clutching at radiators resolutely set at 68 degrees, we welcome April, the harbinger of warm months ahead. For those of us who love a garden, April has a particular magic in its promise of spring and summer flowers. Like most gardeners, I spend the winter months reviewing books and catalogues, planning new borders or additions to my existing flower beds. I also read the horticultural magazines and ecological journals for news about new insecticides and fertilizers. Unlike many gardeners, however, I have qualifications I adhere to rigidly. I eliminate fussy, demanding plants that require a lot of maintenance and devotion. I try to stay away from too much staking, dividing, and other cultural directions that call for more than watering, fertilizing, and cutting back. You see, I am quite lazy. I had hoped to find a less pejorative adjective, but the dictionary lists words like "indolent" and "slothful" which sound even worse. I tried to describe myself as a sybarite or an epicure, but I found out that they ski, and jog, and exercise. So be it. Lazy is the word. Nevertheless, I adore flowers, and I have been successful in cultivating beautiful borders which bloom from spring to fall in a myriad of shapes and colors and do not require more than one or two hours a week, except for the first weekend in the spring and the last one in the fall.

I know what you are thinking. People who own weekend homes always shorten the time it takes to get there by about fifteen minutes when they talk about it. Some gardeners or cooks do the same in describing their hobbies. But remember, this book is not for the serious, dedicated gardener who expects to transform his lot into Westbury Gardens all by himself. It is for those of us who own either a small lot or dozens of acres, but who are unwilling or unable to create one of those picture book gardens. What we want is to grow pretty flowers which bring us pleasure, serenity, and the satisfaction of knowing that we did it ourselves, without sapping all our time, energy, and effort.

I started gardening seven years ago after buying a weekend home in Connecticut. I always admired my friends' and neighbors' gardens, and I bought several books on the subject. By page thirteen, I would lose interest when the work described seemed too time-consuming. One time I actually tied flowers to evergreen shrubs with plastic cord, just to produce a garden. However, I was determined to learn enough about it to create my own flower border, and I stuck to it. Unfortunately, many good books are for those gardeners who devote a great deal of time to their hobby, and the pictures they show are usually taken at estates where additional help is hired. If I had a gardener, and all I had to do is point to where I want the plants, I, too, would have one of those breathtaking flower beds, and I would include many more species. However, I do the work myself and mind it, so I have excluded all but the low-maintenance perennials. Don't feel cheated. There are enough to choose from so that you'll have to omit some, and the pictures are only of gardens that people tend to by themselves. Nevertheless, they all flower profusely all season. I know it can be done. I did it, and I propose to show you how.

This book deals essentially with perennials. I don't eschew annuals. On the contrary, they are most useful and decorative. They look great when grown in containers or used to fill in bare spots in the border. Their almost nonexistent cultural requirements can be summed up by any reliable nursery salesman. But if I have to go to the trouble of bending and planting, I may as well concentrate on perennials, those plants which come up every year. I told you. I'm lazy.

Chapter 1

PARLEZ-VOUS GARDENESE?

Now that you are about to use flowery speech, I want to explain the rationale for this minilexicon. Years ago I admired tall purple flowers that grew in swampy areas alongside the highways, and I was told that they were purple loosestrife. When my enthusiasm for gardening awakened, I combed the catalogues and books for the hybridized perennial plants of the same species. Fortunately, the catalogues also referred to their common name, and I was able to find *lythrum,* one of my favorite perennials, known to most of us as plain old purple loosestrife. Nurseries all list the botanical names rather than the common names, so this list should help you find the proper names in books or catalogues. Besides, cultural directions use words that need some defining even for our rudimentary type of gardening.

Incidentally, it's fun to speak gardenese. Recently, while I was shopping at a nursery, a fellow enthusiast suggested that I try some *coreopsis* in my bed. My perennial spouse was a bit undone, never having learned gardenese, and I must confess that I enjoyed his momentary discomfiture.

Let's not get too serious about this. Just remember that "A rose by any other name . . ."

Common Names	Botanical Names	Common Names	Botanical Names
baby's breath	*Gypsophila*	columbine	*Aquilegia*
balloon flower	*Platycodon*	coral bells	*Heuchera*
basket of gold	*Alyssum*	cowslip	*Primula*
beard tongue	*Pentstemon*	cranesbill	*Geranium*
bee balm	*Monarda*	Cupid's dart	*Catanache*
bellflower	*Campanula*	daylily	*Hemerocallis*
bergamot	*Monarda*	evening primrose	*Oenothera*
bleeding heart	*Dicentra*	flax	*Linum*
bugloss	*Anchusa*	foxglove	*Digitalis*
butterfly weed	*Asclepias*	funkia	*Hosta*
campion	*Lychnis*	gas plant	*Dictamnus*
candytuft	*Iberis*	gayfeather	*Liatris*
cardinal flower	*Lobelia*	globe flower	*Trollius*
Carolina lupine	*Thermopsis*	hens and chicks	*Sempervivum*
catchfly	*Lychnis*	indigo	*Baptisia*
catnip	*Nepeta*	lavender	*Lavandula*

Common Names	Botanical Names	Common Names	Botanical Names
lily of the Nile	*Agapanthus*	stonecrop	*Sedum*
lily of the valley	*Convallaria*	tickseed	*Coreopsis*
meadow rue	*Thalictrum*	windflower	*Anemone*
monkshood	*Aconitum*	yarrow	*Achillea*
Oswego tea	*Monarda*		
pinks	*Dianthus*		
plantain lily	*Hosta*		
sage	*Salvia*		
sea thrift	*Armeria*		
speedwell	*Veronica*		
statice	*Limonium*		

try coreopsis in your bed...

Definitions

annual — A plant that seeds, roots, flowers, and dies in one season.

biennial — A plant that is sown one year, flowers the next year, and dies.

compost — Decomposed vegetable matter. Comes in the form of peat moss, leafmold, manure, all of which add humus to the soil, enabling plants to utilize nutrients.

humus — Decaying vegetable matter necessary for good soil. It aids in the absorption of water and helps nutrients to become available to plants from the soil. It provides air space so the roots are not choked by packed earth and also adds its own plant food through chemicals released. Humus is contained in all manure, peat moss, leafmold, and compost.

leafmold — Rotted leaves

mulch — Generally a mulch is anything that can be added to the surface of the soil to help it retain moisture and prevent weeds. Some mulches add nutrients as they decompose. During the winter a mulch will keep the soil at an even temperature and prevent frost heave from tearing roots.

peat moss — A decomposition of plants used as a soil amendment to hold moisture and provide humus. It also makes the soil more acid and is occasionally used on top of the soil as a mulch to keep weeds down.

perennial — A flowering or foliage plant whose roots live from year to year. In colder climates, the foliage dies in the winter but reappears in the spring. Several perennials also have annual and biennial varieties.

Chapter 2

THE BEST LAID PLANS

Starting a garden takes several months of planning, deciding not only *what* to plant but *where* to plant it. I was lucky. We bought our house in the fall, and I had the whole winter to think about it and to observe what already existed in the way of winter color and early spring bloom. If you can be patient, wait for one whole growing season to pass. Believe me, you'll save money and aggravation. You can always fill in with annuals for some summer color.

Look around you and take inventory. Are there enough evergreens to provide winter color and keep the cold months from becoming a dirge of browns and greys? How about the trees and shrubs? Beautiful old maples and oaks need feeding and occasional pruning. Take care of them because they are so difficult to replace. In the spring and summer, see what comes up and what shape it's in. For our purposes, it is just as important to know what we have to eliminate.

When spring came to our property, I saw some lovely *peonies,* bearded *iris,* and good broadleaf evergreens as foundation plantings. Summer brought no flowers. My initial disappointment turned into satisfaction because I realized that this gave me carte blanche for next season's gardens. By now I had read tomes on the subject, and I was determined to create low-care borders. I found the best source to be catalogues of nurseries within a seventy-five mile radius of my home. Until you are an old hand at it, the rationale is that if it grows within that periphery of your house, it will also grow in your own garden. Neighbors' gardens are also a good source of information about what will grow in your area. Watch those neighbors, though. If they don't have a tan on their faces, only on their arms, most probably they are bending over their gardens for most of the day.

During the first summer, I paced out our property and drew a bird's eye sketch, using our surveyor's map as a guide. I studied each location and took notes on the number of hours of sunshine in each projected border, as well as its proximity to water faucets. This is mandatory unless you don't mind dragging several lengths of heavy hose. I made this mistake, but it has been ameliorated somewhat by the purchase of a hose-winder on wheels.

One thing I did not do, which you must absolutely see to. Check all the projected garden areas in the early spring, right after the first thaw, to make sure they don't turn boggy. Frequently these areas drain well in the summer,

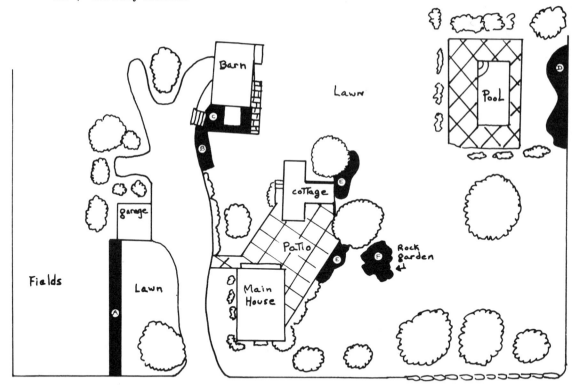

but spring floods ruin all but the most sturdy and deep-rooted plants. To begin with, they cannot tolerate drowning, and secondly, if there is a frost after the thaw, the earth will heave and tear the roots.

The first fall, I filled in section A and started a new border in section B. In A, I just added daylilies and dwarf evergreens to the existing *peonies* and bearded *iris*. I also planted some daffodil bulbs for that breathtaking surprise after winter. The following spring, I added more daylilies and substituted Siberian *iris* for the bearded variety. Although the latter is beautiful, it grows rampant and becomes a host to iris borer which is not only harmful to the plant but is also the most repulsive worm I've ever seen. Now the border, only a few feet wide, is heavily mulched, has the most carefree plants in gardendom, and requires only an annual feeding.

In section B, I planted twelve daylilies of four varieties, which bloom from mid-June to August and need only spring fertilizing. Their arching bladelike foliage is so heavy that no weeding is necessary, and I have even dispensed with the mulching.

Section C is a raised and walled terrace against the stone foundation of a huge barn. The area is about thirty feet long and twelve feet wide. Here, I went crazy and had a mason construct a reflecting pool with a gentle slope of stones in the back. A pump, which is submerged, recirculates the water and sends it cascading over the stones, creating a miniature waterfall. On each side of the pool, I planted magnificent dwarf weeping white pines which admire their reflections in the water. On one side, I added a weeping Japanese cherry tree which is smothered in pink blossoms in the spring. On the other side, I planted a clump of Japanese *iris* which creates an incredibly beautiful display in July. Here, the ground is heavily mulched with pine bark nuggets, and large white stones are placed in a random pattern. Black and white pebbles adorn the bottom of the pool.

Areas A, B, and C are seen as one drives in from the road and also from the patio and the kitchen. In all three I planned for high visibility and low maintenance. Areas marked E are in the shade of two large maples. Here, pachysandra and *hosta* have succeeded well except for two spots, where plants have a quick convulsion and die. After several tries I've given up, and in the summer I place tubs of shade-loving annuals to cover the bare ground.

Section F is a large outcropping of stone. It is boulderlike and irregular. One of the former owners had a mason build little terraces which hold about six inches of topsoil. I used to fill them in with annuals, but they looked unnatural, and last year I planted creeping *phlox* in the terraces and *sedum* and *sempervivum* in the fissures. The *sedum* ruthlessly overtook the entire outcropping except for the pockets of *phlox*. Actually it's quite attractive, so I plan to leave it alone until some fall when I will landscape the area with more perennials and dwarf evergreens. In the section on rock gardening, I include some ideas and a list of perennials suitable for this purpose.

Now we come to section D, and a little biography is in order. When I was growing up, my favorite star was Esther Williams, and I fantasized continually about replacing her as the water queen of Hollywood. In those days only moguls had private swimming pools, so you can imagine that this is my favorite place in the world, and, weather permitting, it's where I spend most of my time. Naturally, that's where I planted my showiest border. This far north of the equator, we swim for only four months — June through mid-September — so I was meticulous in planning for early June through late September bloom. I started this border from scratch, after months of thinking about it. Today it displays a riot of colors in differing shapes, and it flowers continually with very little maintenance because it was so carefully planned. Naturally, I've made some additions and some deletions. Live and learn.

Once you decide where to plant your main flower bed, decide whether you want a long, formal one, or a free-form island. Much depends on the background. Against a hedge or a dry wall or on any boundary line, the long rectangle appears best, and you can make the front irregularly shaped to avoid a look that is too formal. If you are cutting a garden out of the lawn, and you prefer a border that you can walk around, then an island is prettier. A corner can also become a lovely garden. As stated before, you must consider the proximity to faucets, and this could be the deciding factor. In the rectangular bed, the taller plants are against the back, the mid-border plants in the middle, and the edging low-growers in the front. In the islands, the tall ones are in the center, then the mid-border varieties, and the edging plants along the circumference. Remember that many perennials have hybrids that are dwarf, medium height, and very tall, and therefore suitable for many uses.

Your choice will also greatly depend on the hours of sunshine in the area. When the sections suitable for a long, narrow border are in too much shade, the selection of plants is limited, and cutting into the lawn may be necessary to guarantee a full day of sunshine. However, don't become too pedantic about this. Some of the prettiest flowers do their best in partial shade. By shade I mean an area that is hidden from the sun's strongest rays for part or most of the day. By full sun I mean at least seven hours of sunshine daily. All plants need strong light, but a shade-loving plant will do better hidden from the afternoon rays. Conversely, a sun-loving plant will do better exposed to the strong stuff. You'll soon find out that water and healthy soil are much more important than the actual hours of sunbathing. I grow *phlox*, sun worshippers, where they get sun only until two in the afternoon and spend the rest of the day in the dappled shade of a locust tree. They are healthy and very floriferous. The glossary indicates which condition the plants prefer, and there is also a section on plants that actually do better in mostly shady areas.

If you are using a hedge or a wall as a background for your border, plan to leave at least a foot empty behind your background plants. This increases air circulation which prevents fungus, and it also gives your perennials' roots a chance to establish themselves without competing for food and water with the nearby hedges. Drainage is also essential. If the area is too boggy, either build a raised planting bed at least eighteen inches above soil line, or look for another site. The books tell you to "fix" this, but unless you get professional help, you'll regret it. Also think in terms of a raised bed if the site is in an area full of rocks and stones. It could be that four inches under your grass, it is pure ledge. Look elsewhere, but don't become discouraged. Raised borders are elegant, and remember, you don't have to bend as low to work in them. Another bonus is that since you have to fill them anyway, you can buy soil that is just perfect without going through all the corrective measures.

The next thing to decide is when you want the most bloom in the garden and order the bulk of plants for that period. However, be flexible and put some in for earlier as well as later bloom, since our capricious climate can fool you. Plan for large drifts in several colors. Except for some bright oranges, most perennials do not have electric colors, and Mother Nature, liberated lady that she is, made foliage green, and everything seems to blend with that. Shapes count also. Make sure that you have spikes, sprays, clusters, single flowers, and pendulous as well as upright growers. Some of the loveliest vertical turrets look their best when they compete with globe-shaped clusters and large single blossoms. Order at least three of every variety, and plant them together but in irregular patterns. In a woodsy area, try the naturalized garden where plants should be placed as if a bird had dropped the seeds at random, and they just grew there. It is important that foliage remain neat after flowering, so I've eliminated those that don't have that desirable trait.

Before you order, draw a plan. Use graph paper and let each little square represent a foot. Space your plants on one-foot centers, unless the cultural directions state that they need more room. Don't be too methodical about a pattern, and don't plan a border that's too wide, or you'll trample the shorties in the front, trying to reach the biggies in the back. In an island design, try to oblongate the bed so you can have access to the tall ones in the center. Now, use colored pencils to draw the outlines of the sections for each variety. Green pencil should denote the spring plants, red pencil the summer bloomers, and blue the late summer and into fall flowers. Naturally, you should space them so every section of the border has some bloom in it all the time. My favorites are the ones that are outlined in all three colors, showing that they bloom almost all season. You'll see how many of those lovelies are available to the discerning gardener.

As you select plants, make sure you check each variety for height. There are new hybrids emerging all the time. For example, the glossary lists *catanache* which grows to fifteen inches, but a nursery recently developed a new *catanache* that grows two feet tall. Don't order too much right away. As you become more experienced, you'll see that blooming times vary in gardens less than a few hundred feet apart.

You can start a new garden in the spring or in the fall. If you plan to start yours in the fall, prepare the soil in August. For a spring start, prepare the bed in early April. I have found fall planting to be very successful, since it gives roots a chance to establish themselves before the winter. Most plants in this book are suitable for a fall start, unless spring is recommended in the glossary. Some, such as the *peony* and the hybrid lily bulb, should be planted only in the fall.

The next thing you should check is the hardiness zone. I am not including the map of zones which appears in most gardening books and catalogues. It may teach you some geography, but for the purposes of simple gardens, the chart of minimum temperatures is just as good. Check

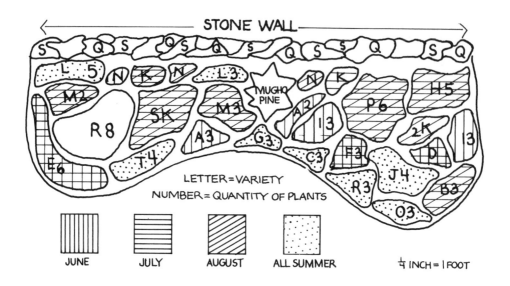

LETTER = VARIETY
NUMBER = QUANTITY OF PLANTS

JUNE   JULY   AUGUST   ALL SUMMER   ¼ INCH = I FOOT

PLAN I

NAME	HEIGHT	COLOR
A) *Aquilegia*	2½ Ft.	White and red
B) *Platycodon*	2 Ft.	Blue or white
C) *Coreopsis*	1 Ft.	Yellow
D) *Dictamnus*	2½ Ft.	Pink or white
E) *Astilbe*	1½ - 2½ Ft.	White, pink, red
F) *Lychnis*	2½ Ft.	Red
G) *Gypsophila*	1½ Ft.	Pink
H) *Heliopsis*	3 Ft.	Yellow
I) *Iris Sibirica*	3 Ft.	White or violet
J) *Valerian*	2½ Ft.	White and pink
K) *Daylily*	2½ - 4 Ft.	Yellow, peach, pink
L) *Lythrum*	3½ Ft.	Purple or pink
M) *Monarda*	2 - 2½ Ft.	White, pink, red, blue
N) *Lilium*	3 - 5 Ft.	Yellow, orange, pink
O) *Oenothera*	1 Ft.	Yellow
P) *Phlox*	2½ - 3½ Ft.	White, pink, red, lilac
Q) *Sempervivum*	3"	Pink
R) *Veronica*	1 - 2 Ft.	White, pink, blue
S) *Sedum*	2 - 4 "	Yellow, pink
T) *Heuchera*	1 - 1½ Ft.	White, pink

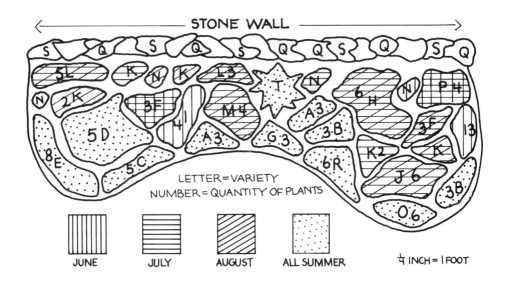

LETTER = VARIETY
NUMBER = QUANTITY OF PLANTS

JUNE JULY AUGUST ALL SUMMER

¼ INCH = 1 FOOT

PLAN II

NAME	HEIGHT	COLOR
A) *Achillea*	1½ - 2 Ft.	White, yellow
B) *Pentstemon*	1½ - 3 Ft.	Pink, orange, blue
C) *Linum*	1 - 2 Ft.	White or blue
D) *Valerian*	2½ Ft.	White or pink
E) *Tradescantia*	1½ - 3 Ft.	White, pink, purple
F) *Campanula*	2½ Ft.	Blue or white
G) *Geranium*	1½ Ft.	Blue or crimson
H) *Heliopsis*	3 Ft.	Yellow
I) *Iris Sibirica*	3 Ft.	Blue or White
J) *Salvia*	2½ Ft.	Purple or blue
K) *Daylily*	2½ - 4 Ft.	Yellow, apricot, red
L) *Thalictrum*	3 Ft.	Lavender
M) *Sidalcea*	2½ Ft.	Rosy pink
N) *Lilium*	3 - 5 Ft.	Yellow, orange, red
O) *Dianthus*	1 Ft.	Pink, red
P) *Thermopsis*	3 Ft.	Yellow
Q) *Alyssum*	6"	Yellow
R) *Veronica*	18"	Blue, white or pink
S) *Tunica*	6"	Pink
T) *Potentilla*	3 Ft.	Yellow

with your town hall or fuel supplier to find out the minimum winter temperature in your area, and remember that zones may vary right within your property. If you are on a promontory, it probably gets colder, and if you are in a valley, the converse may be true. Wind and humidity are also factors which cause differences. All the plants in the glossary will grow throughout most of the United States except where specified.

Minimum Temperatures

Zone   1:   dwellers should consult with Eskimo gardeners

Zone   2:   30 below zero to 40 below

Zone   3:   20 below zero to 30 below

Zone   4:   10 below zero to 20 below

Zone   5:   5 below zero to 10 below

Zone   6:   5 below zero to 5 above

Zone   7:   5 above zero to 10 above

Zone   8:   10 above zero to 20 above

Zone   9:   20 above zero to 30 above

Zone 10:   30 above zero to 40 above

Don't be too rigid about these numbers. Naturally, you can't go too far in either direction in your experimenting, for too much heat is as dangerous as too little for some perennials. The glossary indicates how far north and how far south the plants can prosper. Gamble a little, and give some plants some extra winter protection. You may lose one or two, but the ones you win will become your treasures.

The term, hardiness, always makes me think of a fig tree which I have been coddling for years. I grow it two zones north of the recommended zone. Each winter I cover it with burlap and mulch the base. Each summer I get foliage but no fruit. This past summer my children placed several boxes of dehydrated figs along its base. Delicious, but not home grown. Maybe next year . . .

That about sizes it up for the planning part of it. Buy the tools I recommend in the following chapter, and try to get over your aversion to bugs, dirt, and, if you are like me, to bending and kneeling.

Chapter 3

HANDY TOOLS

Gardening has its key verbs. They are scooping, digging, cultivating, pruning, cutting, watering, and last but not least, cleaning and removing. Each has tools designed specifically for the purpose. Of course, you can go absolutely crazy and buy everything. When I evinced an interest in gardening, my husband, the shopper in our family, bought me absolutely everything. Except for the ones I am going to tell you about, they all hang, new and unused, looking like rejected job applicants, all dressed up and nowhere to go.

Long-handled Tools

Get *two shovels,* one a square end spade for digging, and the other a scoop type for scooping the earth.

A *spading fork* looks like a giant fork with a long handle. It is essential for breaking up the soil in order to work additives into it. It is also excellent for digging up perennials, dividing, or transplanting, since it does not tear the roots easily.

A *cultivator* has four curved tines which loosen the soil without going too deep. It is necessary for weeding and also for working a top dressing of fertilizer into the soil's surface. In addition it will move mulch around without disturbing the roots.

Get *two rakes,* one a steel garden rake for working in the soil, and the other a bamboo rake for clearing debris and leaves from the border and surrounding areas.

Short-handled Tools

For working on your hands and knees — there isn't any other way —

get a few *trowels* for digging. Make sure that the handles are wooden or covered with plastic so they don't cut into your palms.

A small *hand cultivator* and an asparagus or *dandelion weeder* help when you are doing work around the crowns of the plant or under arching foliage.

Cutting Back and Pruning

The most essential cutting tool is a short-handled, simple *pruning shears.* It is used for cutting roots when dividing plant stock, for thinning and cutting back foliage and flowers, for removing faded blossoms, and for opening heavy bags of fertilizer or soil additives.

Get a longer *lopping shear* for reaching perennials or shrubbery in the back of the border, without having to trample over the plants.

Watering and Spraying

Garden hoses come in different sizes and materials. Go for the good, expensive ones that come with a warranty for long wear. The hoses are available in fifty- or sixty-foot lengths. If you will be watering

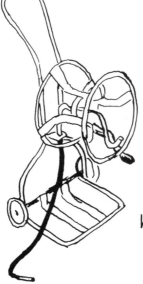

hose winder reel

The easiest border in the world is one comprised of several varieties of daylilies.

areas farther away, get two with a connector, and make sure you get a winder-reel to store, as well as to wind the hoses. The best hoses are made of

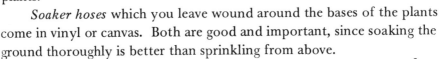

rubber and vinyl with a diameter of 5/8 of an inch. Each faucet should have a hose for it, and each hose should have its own pistol nozzle that allows you to vary the flow from a hard rush to a fine spray.

A *fan nozzle* is also good for watering large areas and container plants.

Soaker hoses which you leave wound around the bases of the plants come in vinyl or canvas. Both are good and important, since soaking the ground thoroughly is better than sprinkling from above.

For spraying insecticide or fungicide, get one *hand sprayer* for spot work and a *hose end sprayer* for large areas. The hose end spray-ers are the most useful, and they automatically proportion the amount of chemicals added to the water. I keep two of these. One is used for insecticides and the other is used for fertilizing container plants and shrubbery. After using them, clean thoroughly before storing.

Cleaning and Moving

The last indispensable item you need is a good, sturdy, easy-to-move *wheelbarrow.* No need to describe the many uses you'll find for it. I even use mine to mix potting soil. If your gardening chores are finished, and you find yourself inspired, you may even use it to give a youngster a fun ride.

Chapter 4

THE NITTY GRITTY

getting into the nitty gritty

Perennial plants are meant to come up every year for many years. Although much of their life expectancy depends on proper maintenance, the initial preparation of their permanent home is most important. Established gardens can be refurbished, but if you do it right the first time, you will never need to repeat it.

When you first thrust the spading fork into the ground, don't be discouraged if the soil comes up a globby, sticky mess which forms a hard lump in the palm of your hand. On the other hand, it may be a crumbly mess which does not adhere at all. Soil should be a thick, dark, rich loam which will support roots firmly, but malleable enough to let the roots dig in and spread out. This is called friable soil. It really means workable.

Spray a hard rush of water on the soil, and see whether it puddles or pours through quickly, leaving the top sandy and crumbly. Well-prepared soil should not do either. It should not form puddles, and it should remain

I can't talk ... I'm mulching

moist for hours after watering. Don't panic. There are corrective additives which will make the soil drain well and remain friable.

If you have a work ethic that promises rewards in an afterlife for back-breaking work, do-it-yourself with the proper tools and work in the soil "fixers." But, if you bought this book, you want the easier way. The results are the same.

Make a date with a friendly Rototiller man. Before he comes, spread a thick layer of peat moss, manure, builders' sand, and a sprinkling of 5-10-5 (five pounds per 100 square feet) fertilizer over the area set aside for your border. If the soil was too crumbly, go heavy on the peat moss, and conversely, if it was too gloppy, use a little more sand. Then, when the tiller comes, he will churn all the ingredients into the ground. Water thoroughly and observe the improvements. The soil should be of a better consistency and ready for planting.

The peat moss and manure act as humus. This is the end product of decomposing vegetable matter which makes the soil porous and hospitable to your plants. The fertilizer contains nitrogen, phosphate, and potassium in proportionate amounts, which promote leaf growth, root growth, and sturdy stems and branches. If you want to know more about the specific way they act, ask a botanist. Otherwise take it from me. It's good for your plants. The sand keeps the soil from getting lumpy by creating air spaces.

Before we continue, let's have a word about sweet versus acid soil. In all likelihood, your soil is neutral to slightly acid, a condition that most of the plants in this book welcome. As a matter of fact, some of them actually suffer when the soil is too sweet or alkaline. Buy yourself the simplest testing kit and check the pH of the soil. A neutral reading shows 6.5 to 7. Below that is acid and above that is alkaline. If your soil is slightly acid, leave it alone. If it is very acid, ground limestone mixed in with your second rototilling will correct it. If it is alkaline, give it an extra helping of peat moss, or add aluminum sulphate. Don't be a stickler for perfect neutrality. When the cultural directions for plants state that they prefer an alkaline soil, you can always add a little limestone around their roots. If, on the other hand, they hate lime the way heathers and Japanese *iris* do, you can always work in more peat moss around them. Again, and I'll tell you this often, don't be too pedantic. Leave the chemistry to the chemists, and make gardening a hobby, not an obsession. Just add the correctives, and remember that soils do have a tendency to revert to their original pH, so you may have to add peat or limestone every five years or so.

One week after the first tilling, add another round of the soil "fixers" to the topsoil, and let the Rototiller do its thing again. By now, I promise you that the soil is ready for planting. Alas, the proof is in the proliferation

Peonies *are the sturdiest, most carefree perennials in any garden.*

of lush weeds. Since mulching is a must for our low-care borders, it's never too soon to spread it over the garden area. The section on maintenance goes into the types of mulch in detail. Whichever you choose, put a good layer over the surface of the soil. When the plants arrive, you can always move it aside to start digging.

Peonies and hybrid lilies require some special directions for planting which we will go into later, but for the most part, the rule is to dig a hole deeper and wider than the present roots. If you ordered plants by mail, most of them will arrive bare-rooted with moist peat moss around them. Shake off the peat, and dip the roots into a bucket filled with water. Then place them into the hole with one hand, while fanning them out with the other hand. Replace the soil around the roots firmly, making sure there are no air pockets. The crown of the plant, the center section from which the foliage and stems arise, should be level with the soil line. After the plants are in, use your bare feet or the palm of your hand to tamp in the surrounding soil so the plants are well supported. If you have purchased container-grown stock, shake them out of the container, and loosen the earth around the roots. I always dip them in the handy water bucket before planting to make sure they have not gotten root bound or dried out. If you have a lot of planting to do, it's a good idea to keep the plants in the shade in a flat of water or wrapped in soaking wet rags. It's unbelievable how quickly they can dry up when exposed to the sun.

After planting, gingerly replace the mulch around the bases, leaving enough room for spreading. When this is done, give the garden a thorough soaking. Try to place large stones, bricks, or an extra helping of mulch about six inches in front of the border so the grass will not be incursive. If you have a straight edge, railroad ties are most effective, but they have to be dug in so they don't obscure the low-growing edging perennials.

I know how impatient you are, but don't plant too soon. Most reliable nurseries will not send stock before a safe planting time, but use your judgment when buying container-grown plants. If the weather is threatening, and it is still possible that a hard frost is on the way, keep the containers moist, and wait for a better day. A heavy downpour is also detrimental to newly planted perennials, since the soil needs a few days to settle down after planting. If a storm occurs right after you planted, when it's over, check the garden, and tamp the ground again around each perennial. Cold and water are good for plants, but acute changes are not, especially for young ones.

Another symptom of impatience is planting too close together. It only means more work. The glossary indicates which plants need more than a square foot, but for most plants, twelve inches is enough room. At first it will look sparse, but perennials spread and grow, and planting them closer will force them to compete with one another for the soil's nutrients. It will also encourage breeding of insects, and growth and spread of fungus and disease.

Don't expect too much the first season, no matter how well you have followed instructions, and no matter how extravagant the claims of the nurseries are. Fill in with annuals for summer color, and next year your patience will be rewarded.

Oh, and another thing. Don't add more fertilizer, hoping for better results. Instead, make sure you keep the garden clean of weeds, free of the bad bugs, and covered with mulch.

Chapter 5

BRINGING UP PERENNIALS

"As ye sow, so shall ye reap." Would it were so. No matter how well you have sown, the care is ongoing and necessary to reap the rewards. In gardenese, there are some key verbs. They are watering, weeding, mulching, staking, thinning, cutting back, dividing and transplanting, feeding, wintering, and two new verbs, "insecticiding" and "fungiciding."

First, we'll get to the easy one we think we know all about. Every living thing needs water, and perennials need at least an inch a week. Drowning is not the idea here; therefore, hoping that two inches at one time will carry the plant over for two weeks is out of the question and sometimes terminal.

The roots provide for the plant, so they must get the most water. Sprinkling lightly from overhead, for a few minutes, every so often, is like giving your plants the Chinese water drop torture. First of all, it encourages the roots to form near the surface of the soil where they'll get mauled by the lightest cultivation. Secondly, by keeping the garden moist, it creates the perfect ambiance for insects and fungus.

Soil should be wet to a depth of about eight inches, but the foliage of the plants should remain dry. The best way to do this is to leave a plastic or canvas soaker hose coiled around the bases of the plants, with the holes facing downwards. A few stones should be placed under the hose every foot or so, to make sure that the holes do not get clogged. Attach a hose from your faucet to the soaker, open the valve, and do other chores while your border is getting a good drink of water.

After a protracted dry spell, you can give the foliage a good washing to remove dust, but always do it in the late afternoon, after the strong sun has abated, or in the early morning. Sprinkling in the hot sun is never a good idea. To begin with, evaporation takes away much of the needed water, and secondly, as stated before, it encourages fungus.

Don't throw away a worn hose. Punch holes in it, and use it as a soaker hose. By placing stones or pieces of bark over the holes, you can deflect the water towards the soil. If the foliage of your plants is thick and lush, it should conceal the hose anyway, and you can leave it there all season.

I always like to quote Amos Pettingill, the guru of White Flower Farm. About watering he suggests, "Keep their feet wet, and their bonnets dry."

One caution I'll add to that. Pool water contains chemicals which keep it sparkling and clean but are deadly to plants. Remember that.

Weeding is conducive to backaches and disillusion about gardening. Unfortunately, the better the soil is prepared, the more weeds there are to pull out. If your work schedule and lumbosacral column permit weeding carefully every ten days or so, you can generally control the problem, but why not avoid it? Mulching, which really means covering the surface of the soil to inhibit weeds, is the answer.

While proper mulching reduces your work load, it also conserves the moisture in the soil, coaches the roots to develop correctly, protects the plants from frost heave, breaks down and adds nutrition to the soil, and looks attractive. What drawback can something that beneficial have? It's that the best mulch is also the most expensive. By best I mean evergreen bark nuggets or chips. Their brown color looks lovely with foliage green and blends with the color of soil. They last for a very long time and need renewing only intermittently; they can't be washed away or blown away in a storm; removing leaves in the fall hardly disturbs them. A long-handled cultivator redistributes them with no trouble. Some things are worth the extra money, and this is one of them. You can also cut down on the expense by putting a bottom layer of shredded wood chips on first and saving the redwood chips for the top. Garden experts tell you that since the chips don't rot easily, they leach nitrogen from the soil and aren't as nutritive as other mulches. I just give the garden a few extra feedings of fertilizer a season, and I have not had any trouble.

Other mulching materials are peat moss, leafmold, grass clippings, ground corncobs, and buckwheat hulls. Peat moss tends to dry and cake so that water runs off it instead of into it. Leafmold has to be screened for insects, or it may bring an epidemic to your garden. Grass clippings tend to get matted and dry, but for a shallow border or "pocket garden," they are fine and no trouble to locate if you have a lawn. Buckwheat hulls are not bad looking, but I have found them too light and easily blown or washed away, as well as very expensive. That brings us back to bark chips which get my vote.

Whichever mulch you use, always make sure that you apply the most in the areas between the plants, gradually tapering it toward the bases. Leave a bare section around the crowns to avoid rot and to permit growth and spread. Always bear in mind that large chips look silly next to the smaller plants in the rock garden or in the forefront of the border, whereas they look best around tall, bushy plants in the back, so buy some of each size.

When you plant in the fall, leave markers to indicate where you expect growth the following spring. Be cautious when you do weed around a mulched area. Until you are more experienced, you may be pulling out some valuable plants. Use the time you are saving to learn more about gardening, and soon you'll be giving advice.

Staking plants is not an onerous chore, but I prefer to buy varieties that don't need it. I find the appearance of tall sticks in the garden annoying, unattractive, and reminiscent of a vegetable lot. *Peonies* are lovely flowers, easy to grow, and easy to care for, so they are worth the extra effort. The best and easiest way to stake them, as well as other bushy plants, is to place a three-leg circular wire stand around their crowns in the early spring. Their foliage will soon conceal the support. Tall, leggy plants, such as some of the hybrid lilies, should be staked to wire or bamboo sticks placed closely behind them. Where several perennials of the same height grow close together, one stake will suffice for all three. Always tie them loosely so they are not strangled, and keep the stake lower than the foliage.

Some wiry and pendulous plants can be supported by concealing twigs and branches under their foliage and letting the stems arch over. There are more sophisticated ways to do this, but it is almost tantamount to "corset-ting" them, so avoid it. By checking the heights carefully, you can limit staking to those flowers whose beauty and length of bloom make them indispensable.

staking plants

Thinning bushy plants is very important for two reasons. It prevents fungus growth by providing better air circulation, and it induces stronger stems which are more floriferous. During the very early spring growth, cut several shoots down to the crown, leaving only three or four at most. You may find this hard to do at first, convinced that more stems mean more flowers. It only means weaker flowers on droopy, tumbling stems. You see, the roots have to provide the strength for the stalks; consequently, fewer stalks will get more of the nourishment. It seems so elementary once you learn it.

After flowering cut off all the flower heads before they go to seed. This, too, is related to saving the roots' energies, and the frequent reward is a second crop of blossoms. In the case of some hybridized flowers like *phlox*, it also prevents the growth of seedlings which ungratefully smother the mother plant and revert to the uninteresting colors and forms of the original wildflowers. Besides, a garden looks neater when rid of spent blossoms. If the blooming season for a particular plant is really over, you may cut further down into the foliage. However, leave enough stems and leaves so the plant looks alive until fall when the stems should be cut down to the crown.

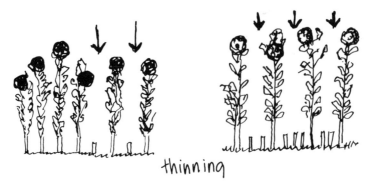

thinning

Transplanting or moving a plant becomes necessary when you want to enlarge a garden or change a pattern. Recently, I moved several *phlox* and *heliopsis* whose unforseen height was obscuring some lovely flowers behind them. The best way to do this is to dig a trench around the base of the plant. Make it a wide circle, about one foot deep. Use a spade to do it. Then scoop out the entire plant with a spading fork, keeping as much of the soil around the roots as possible. Don't do it in too much of a hurry. "Tease" the plant out so you don't tear too many roots. Before you attempt it, make sure that you have prepared another hole in advance, since it's never a good idea to keep the plants out of the soil for too long. Some perennials react poorly to moving about and are best left undisturbed. The glossary tells you which ones, but for the most part, they can be moved anytime, even when in bloom. I personally prefer doing it in the fall or very early spring. When transplanting is done after flowering, always cut the foliage down to about three inches above the crown so that the roots can concentrate on establishing their new "digs." Water thoroughly after moving.

After a few years in the garden, some plants tend to overrun and crowd out others. Some perennials form large clumps, but their blooming period gets shorter, and the quality of their flowers diminishes. In both cases it's time to dig up the plants and divide the roots. This procedure is also a form of propagation, and one large and favorite plant can be turned into several by proper separation and replanting of roots. The best time to do it is in the very early spring or in the fall after flowering has stopped.

The first step is to dig up the plant, as described for transplanting. Use a pistol nozzle, and hose away the surrounding soil so you can see what you're doing. Some perennials have very shallow roots which will practically fall into divisions by themselves, but others have thick, fibrous roots which are intertwined and impossible to pull apart. To divide these, thrust two spading forks, back to back, into the center of the roots, and pull them apart until they pry the plant into two sections. Don't worry about tearing some roots. Plants that require this are very sturdy and will not be hurt by it.

Keep the divisions fairly broad, since it takes two seasons before they grow
large again. Perennials like *heliopsis* and *phlox* have long whiskery roots
with new growth on the periphery of an older, woody center. These should
be divided by cutting the new growth for replanting and discarding
the wasted center. Use a knife or a pruning shear to do this, and always
make sure that you leave a sizeable division. In all cases, before replacing
the plant, refurbish the soil a bit, and plant the new divisions firmly.
Cut down the foliage if you do it in the fall. In the spring, trim the plant
somewhat. Those plants for which only spring planting is recommended
should be divided only in the spring, and conversely, fall plantings divided
only in the fall. Always water thoroughly after surgery.

Dividing is not difficult, but if you
have too many plants, it can become a
hateful chore, and the tendency is to
let the plants go. There are many
lovely perennials that never, or hardly
ever, need separating. Try to plant as
many of these as possible so you can
give the extra attention to the aristocrats whose beauty and long season of
bloom are worth the additional care.

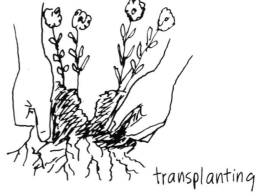

transplanting

As I mentioned earlier, plants
need nitrogen, phosphate, and potash, each for a good reason. Fertilizers
are prepared, stating the percentage of each in the same order. For example,
the formula we use, 5-10-5, indicates the presence of 5 per cent nitrogen,
10 per cent phosphate, and 5 per cent potash. Many garden manuals tell you
to use superphosphate which means more phosphate. By using the formula
5-10-5, you are doing this automatically. A well-established garden, in good
soil, needs two feedings a year, one in early spring and one in late June. I
always add an extra shot of fertilizer in August because I use pine bark chips
as a mulch. A twenty-five-pound bag of fertilizer is the most you will need.
It should be used at the rate of two pounds per 100 square feet, or a sprinkling of it around the base of each plant. I just broadcast the dry powder, trying to avoid the foliage, and cultivate it lightly into the topsoil. After
watering thoroughly, replace the mulch that has been moved aside. For the
second or third feedings, I don't even move the mulch aside. Just a spray of
the powder, some quick superficial cultivating, and a good dose of water does
the trick. One caution about overfeeding — it's bad for your spouse, bad for
your kids, bad for your pets, and bad for your plants.

If you take care of your garden, the soil should remain rich and plant-
worthy. I refurbish my garden a bit every other spring. Move the mulch

toward the back or away from the forefront, and work a top dressing of peat moss and dehydrated cow manure into the surface of the soil. If you have a compost heap, now is the time to work the humus into your garden. Add a toss of fertilizer for good luck, cultivate, replace the mulch, and water.

When it comes to "insecticiding" and "fungiciding," I always solemnly recommend the non-chemical approach first. Careful thinning, garden hygiene, proper watering, and encouraging nature's little helpers, like the praying mantis and the ladybug, should keep your plants insect-and disease-free. Well, the good bugs will not get all the bad guys, and the fungus will still appear, unless you go for the chemicals. Ecologists now use the word "control" cautiously, since many of the chemicals that eradicate insects are also highly toxic to other living things. You have to be cautious, too, and keep abreast of new developments. Remember that DDT was used widely before it was taken off the market, so anything I recommend today may be judged too highly toxic in a year, or may be replaced by something better. Do your homework, and read horticultural and ecological journals.

Insects spend their time chewing foliage or sucking the sap and strength from the leaves. The chewers leave tiny holes on the bitten leaves. They are beetles, leaf miners, borers, snails, and slugs. The last two can be lured to a bacchanalian death by your placing shallow bowls of beer near the plants and letting them drown in a drunken stupor. If they are doing heavy damage, use sprays recommended by a reliable nursery or a local conservation group. For the other chewers, use carbaryl, available commercially as Sevin. The suckers are aphids, thrips, spider mites, and leaf hoppers. They can be controlled by a hard rush of water to knock them off the leaves, followed by the use of malathion. These nasty suckers cause the leaves to become stippled, curled, or discolored.

Carbaryl and malathion are compatible for use together. Read the instructions on the label, and follow them rigidly, using a hose end sprayer which automatically proportions the water being added to the chemicals. Always add a "sticker" which makes the insecticide adhere to the leaves. Direct the spray so that it coats the underside of the foliage, as well as the top growth.

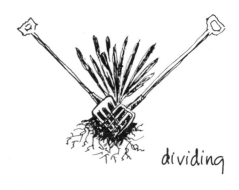

dividing

Fungus or leaf disease is described as blight, powdery mildew, or downy mildew. Fungus often seen on *phlox* is unsightly but not dangerous to the plant. However, other forms of the disease may kill some perennials. The first step is to remove all damaged stems and leaves, and then spray with

Campanula carpatica *is a great rock garden plant, and like all* campanulas, *a low-maintenance perennial.*

ferbam, folpet, captan, benomyl, or Bordeaux mixture. I use benomyl, which can be added to the insecticide, as long as the "sticker" is added last of all.

There are commercial preparations that contain fungicide, as well as insecticide. If you wish to save time, you can use these broad-spectrum mixtures. I personally prefer to mix my own. Because I know that all chemicals are potentially dangerous, I feel more secure using the ones I mentioned. In the spring, I use a prophylactic mixture of the insecticide and fungicide. During the rest of the season, I spray every ten days or so. If one problem seems more acute than the others, I use whichever chemical is called for, without adding the others. Play it by ear, but don't go for overkill. For some reason that is clear only to entymologists, it only aggravates the condition.

Speaking of bugs, you know they don't attack only plants, so dress correctly. One time I decided that my back needed some tanning, so I performed my chores in a bathing suit. Two nasty bees had a field day, and since then, I always wear long sleeves and pants. Gloves help too, unless you model for the "before" shots of hand cream ads.

As sure as summer comes, so shall winter, and a few preparations are in order. If you have tall, deciduous trees on your property, you'll have fallen leaves. Unless they are oak leaves, which make a good mulch, remove them. Maple and locust leaves tend to mat and smother the plants. Cut all the foliage down to a few inches above the crown, and keep the garden watered until frost. In late December, cover the recently planted perennials and the less hardy ones with evergreen boughs. Don't suffocate them; just protect them. If your garden is shielded from strong winds, and you get a nice coat of snow, don't make too much of winter protection the second season. If you've strayed a bit in the hardiness zone, pamper only those plants every year. It's miraculous how perennials can survive even the harshest winters. Some of them, like *peony* and Siberian *iris,* actually seem to thrive in the cold. Relax, go sit in front of the fireplace or radiator, and buy some more books on this lovely subject. By now, you may be planning to write *The Not So Lazy Gardener.* If you have a fireplace, save those wood ashes for the *peonies.*

Now I've told you most of what I know about maintenance, and possibly, more than you want to know. Let me caution you in advance that sometimes, even if you follow every instruction to the letter, some of your plants will still look like measly relatives of some of your neighbors' prizewinners. Ask them for special hints. All I've ever gotten is something similar to a recipe from a mother-in-law. I just know some secret is being kept.

Another suggestion I feel compelled to make: Some plants do die; let them. Don't ministrate too much, hoping to revive them. Just keeping the roots wet will encourage new growth which will mislead you into expecting a miraculous revival. Pull them out, get some new ones, and save the heroics. It's fun to add new plants, anyway.

Chapter 6

POT LUCK

This book is really for those who want to garden with perennials. But who can resist the sight of several pots of annuals massed near a gate, or on a terrace, or suspended from the branches of trees? Container gardening is a happy extension of the ground-level stuff, and you can move potted plants around, creating instant gardens. When we have company for dinner on the patio, I bring all my potted plants into the area. The compliments for the food go to Colonel Sanders, but I modestly accept the plaudits for the lovely flowers.

The choice of sizes, materials, types, and colors is endless, and if you or your spouse likes carpentry, you can make your own containers. I personally perfer the standard clay pots for standing containers and plastic ones for hanging. They are both easy to clean and store, and they also look good around colonial or space-age architecture. Half barrels or antique reproductions of urns are also attractive, though somewhat harder to move.

Container plants have a small plot to grow in, so they can't forage for food and drink. Therefore, it is very important that their soil be of the highest quality. I buy prepared potting soil which is always insect-free and of the proper consistency, and I throw in a potful of bonemeal to every twenty-five-pound bag. If you insist on mixing your own soil, use spadefuls of good loam, and add builders' sand or vermiculite, and finely ground peat moss, until you are satisfied with the quality. Always line the bottom of the pot with clean pebbles or pieces of broken clay, to provide drainage. Start filling the container until the pebbles are completely covered. Shake the plant free of surrounding soil so the roots fan out a bit, carefully fill the pot, and firm the soil around the roots. When the plants are potted, cover the soil around them with some fine peat moss.

Container plants need to be watered thoroughly about twice a week except in prolonged hot weather. Mass them together, and use the fan sprinkler on your hose, keeping the spray gentle. Water until it comes out through the bottom or pours off the drip pan. Use 5-10-5 in water soluble form every two weeks on all potted plants. If insects or fungi become a problem, place the plants in front of the perennial border, and spray them.

If you place several pots of cascading white petunias on a graduated planter, or terrace them on steps, they give a lovely show, and they almost shine in the dark. Impatiens, hanging from a shady branch or awning, are beautiful, and a half barrel loaded with them in a shady corner is unforgettable. In fact many low-growing annuals such as ageratum, pansies, and annual *alyssum* are suitable for mobile homes. But, alas, comes winter, and you have to say goodby, and wash and store the pots till next year.

There are, however, four splendid container plants that can be wintered without too much fuss. Let me tell you about them.

Fuchsia is a shade-loving plant which is memorable for its drooping flowers in lovely shades of pink, red, and purple, frequently contrasted with each other, or with white. It has petals on the outside and tubular centers. When fertilized every two weeks and properly watered, it will bloom profusely from June until October. The foliage is dark green and pendulous, and, except for plants grown as trees, fuchsia looks best in a hanging container.

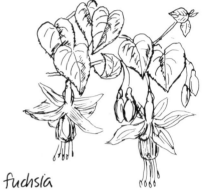

fuchsia

Lantana grows in clusters of tiny florets which cap deeply lobed, dark green, mintlike foliage. The colors are white, yellow, orange, red, and bright pink. Each cluster has a center grouping of florets in one color, with the circumference in a contrasting or darker shade. White lantana is rare and not as striking. The pendulous variety comes in a beautiful shade of mauve. Lantanas need plenty of water, lots of sun, and a dose of fertilizer every other week. They bloom all summer long, and form berries in the fall.

lantana

Both lantana and fuchsia are not hardy in the north, and they grow haggard and scraggly when treated as house plants. However, Mr. Amos Pettingill of White Flower Farm told me how to winter them, and they are now on their fourth season. Try it. In October, bring them indoors and prune severely. When I saw how skeletal I had made them, I had the same reaction I have after I go to the hairdresser for a trim and wind up with an inch of hair. After this radical surgery, store them in an attic or basement where the temperature stays between 40 and 50 degrees. Water them every two weeks or so, just enough to keep the wood from drying out. In late February, bring them into the house, and set them near a sunny window. Water once a week, and as soon as new leaves start to bud, perform your "stemectomy" again, pruning down almost to the crown. Both of these plants flower only on new wood, so don't be alarmed. When growth starts again, repot them. If you want them to grow, go into the next size container. When they get as large as you want them to remain, prune the roots and replant them in the same pot. You can even start training them as trees, but unless you have a greenhouse, this is difficult to do. I prefer keeping mine the same size. Both do well in standard potting soil, and as soon as all danger of frost is past, I pinch them back a bit and bring them outdoors.

Agapanthus, or lily of the Nile, is a marvelous container plant, perfectly suited for a sunny place on the patio or near a pool. They have lilylike arching foliage which hangs over the side of the container. Tall, sturdy stems rise above the leaves, bearing clusters of blue or white flowers. They bloom all of July and August. There are dwarf, as well as tall varieties, equally handsome. They are heavy drinkers and grow quickly, so dividing the roots is necessary. In October, bring them indoors, and let them

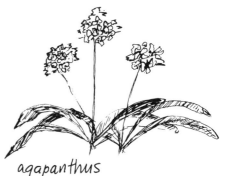

agapanthus

ride out the winter on a window sill. Just keep them watered, and feed them every month. In the spring, repot them, and increase watering and fertilizing until it's warm enough to bring them out again. For something so beautiful, they're amazingly easy to care for.

Another showy plant for a large tub or half barrel is the bedder dahlia. The tall dahlias are sensational, but they are too tall and need staking. The smaller varieties are just beautiful, and from early July until frost, they reward you with continous bloom in bright shades of yellow, orange, red, and pink. They need plenty of water, lots of sun, and the usual dose of food. You start dahlias from tubers, which are planted with the small sprouts facing up-

dahlia

wards, from two to four inches deep, depending on the type you buy. Use regular potting soil, and add a little vermiculite. If you start them indoors, they will bloom earlier, but don't rush them outside. They are very susceptible to the cold.

When you spray malathion on your perennial border, give the dahlias a bit too, since aphids seem to love them. Cut off spent blossoms to induce continuous flowering. When frost comes, leave them out for a few days; then cut down to the crown, and dig up the

dividing dahlia tubers

tubers. Wash them carefully, and let them dry in the sun. Store them in plastic bags with moist vermiculite and peat moss. In the spring, divide the tubers with a knife, making sure to leave buds on each one, and replant them.

People who are houseguests frequently wonder what to bring their hosts. Unlike the proverbial coals, plants are always welcome to a gardener. A pot of fuchsia or lantana, a started dahlia, or an *agapanthus* makes an excellent gift. One of each guarantees more invitations. Instead of writing out the usual platitudes on the gift card, write the directions for wintering. Any host would be delighted and impressed.

Creeping phlox, *ferns and primroses, and voila, a rock garden from a boulder.*

Chapter 7

ON THE ROCKS

If your site is loaded with large stones, boulders, and solid ledge a few inches below the grass, or if you have enormous outcroppings of massive stone breaking up the lawn, don't panic. Believe it or not, these can be turned into an asset. So can an incline that's too steep to mow, or a dry wall that looks dull and gray. Like other things, gardening, too, can be fun "on the rocks." By now, you know well enough that I don't mean one of those impressive, colossal, demanding backgrounds, with water rushing through immortal stones, in a setting like Easter Island. What I really mean is an informal setting that shows you can work with nature, one that challenges your ingenuity and creative spirit. Did you ever notice how the granite hills, through which some of our highways are cut, are dotted with shrubs and trees? Plants will grow out of what appears to be solid rock, from inside the tiniest crevices. Vines that climb hundreds of feet grow out of just inches of soil, and even trees will cling to the sides of cliffs, their roots tortuously digging into small pockets of earth.

try flowers on the rocks...

The real "mavens" on rock gardening smugly make distinctions between rock gardens which are settings where only rock plants are grown, and rockeries, which are large stoneworks planted with any varieties. Frankly, to me it's all the same, namely, an effort to place stone and plant together, to create an environment that is beautiful and harmonious in its utilization of space and mass, while maintaining the utmost informality. A rock garden should look as if it had happened without man's interference, centuries ago. It sounds lofty, but simply and properly done, it captures that look and keeps it without too much in the way of maintenance.

A boulder's hollows or fissures should be filled with a little soil and sand and planted with *sedum* and *sempervivum*. *Sedum* has come to us from the Latin *sedo* meaning to sit. You can find about fifty varieties, including the yellow *sedum* acre,

with fleshy leaves and tiny roots. One small planting of it will overtake a boulder easily, but all you have to do to control it is just tear it out. There are several less rampant types which form dark green, attractive covers over stone. Many of them flower with tiny blossoms in red or yellow, but their really distinguishing feature is the speedy growth of vinelike foliage that sustains itself with no care. The *sempervivum* are hens and chicks, fleshy green rosettes tinged with pink, which set out large colonies with minimum care. Some of them have bizarre flowers which extend on fleshy stems from the center. Like *sedum,* they may be too much of a good thing, but for low care, they go unchallenged. If the hollows are deep enough for about four inches of soil, try creeping *phlox.* In the spring, the prostrate, needlelike, evergreen foliage creates a carpet of color with its tiny flowers in pinks and purples.

If there are actual planting pockets between outcroppings, you can also try growing some annuals. I think they are too greenhousy for a rockery, but they are certainly easy enough to care for.

Another possibility for rock gardening is on an incline. The soil should be prepared as for a border, but deeper and with more sand on the bottom. If you can arrange to have a large boulder placed deeply into the soil, so much the prettier. Stones

Hosta *and* astilbe *are essentials in a shady garden walk.*

should not be quarried and regular looking. They should be native to your area. Each stone should be embedded deeply into the soil, with only one-third exposed. Place them irregularly, avoiding a landscaped, geometric look, but ensuring firm plateaus of soil between them which will support plants. Tilt the tops of the stones slightly backward. Before you plant anything, soak the area, and wait for the soil to settle. If possible, wait and see what happens after a heavy rain. Once you ascertain that drainage is good, that the pattern suits you, and that the rock garden will survive a really bad storm, start to plant. Don't make a mixed salad of a dozen plants. Pick a few varieties, and order several of each kind. Try to keep them in proportion to each other and to the stones. As a rule, avoid perennials which grow taller than fifteen inches. Remember that some of your favorite plants are available in dwarf hybrids which are suitable for a rock garden. As in everything else, stick to the undemanding ones, water and feed them, and enjoy them. Mulching may not be necessary if you use creeping plants or those that cover the ground with low foliage or arching branches.

The other possibility for rock gardening is a dry or unmortared wall. Generally, these were built to retain banks, or to demarcate boundaries. Without any planting, they look lovely along a wooded trail but barren and dull in a garden. Since they are informal stackings of unevenly shaped and sized stones, there are many grooves and chinks between them. If you judiciously place some soil in these pockets, you can easily grow *sedum* or *sempervivum* in them. Just cover the roots with about two inches of soil, and watch them spread. If the wall is not too tall, you can create a whole garden on top of it by loading depressions and hollows with soil. If you don't find a ready-made plant pocket, just remove one of the top stones and create one. Here you can plant a whole variety of creeping and trailing plants which will curtain the wall with color. The three most popular plants for grooves in dry walls are *alyssum,* commonly known as basket of gold, *aubretia,* and *arabis.* They all bloom in spring, cascading over the stones. The three are also suited for the front of borders, or for rock gardens on an incline.

Use your judgement in picking plants for a dry wall. Obviously, there are instances where it is impossible to grow anything in the crevices. When looking through catalogues, look for words like *saxatilis* which means growing among rocks, and *muralis* which means growing on walls.

Dwarf evergreen shrubs are something all rock garden enthusiasts should "spruce up" on. They look impressive, casually standing guard near a boulder, or in front of a wall, or at the base of an incline. Another bonus is that they make winter doldrums tolerable because they are what their name tells you, always green.

The broadleaf evergreens and shrubs compete with the flowering trees in early spring, which to me means April 15th, regardless of the official dates. However, I have to caution you that using more than a few of these calls for a rigorous pruning schedule, which is not for us sybarites. How about a low-maintenance rockery, or glen, or hedge of dwarf coniferous evergreens that looks lovely all year, grows into interesting shapes without pruning, and changes colors with the seasons. I knew you'd be interested, so although these plants do not rightly belong listed among perennials, their versatility and carefree nature make them a must for your rock gardens or around your flower borders.

The word "dwarf" is really deceptive here, since not all of them are small enough to belong in dwarfdom. I bought a dwarf Alberta spruce which grows to fifteen feet. However, when compared to the great Alberta spruces which are skyscrapers, it is a midget.

The word I look for when I purchase dwarf evergreens is *nana,* following the botanic name. *Nanas* grow as tall as six feet, but most of them stay at around two to four feet. Always check their ultimate heights and spreads. There are several nurseries that specialize in dwarf conifers, and all will give you this cultural information. You may, if you wish, contain their growth or change their shape by light pruning. Thus, although a weeping hemlock can grow to fifteen feet undisturbed, careful pruning will keep it low. Left alone, some upright or pendulous growers will assume bizarre shapes. I have trees that have grown "hunchbacks" with some extended arms. I like the weird way they look, and they cast marvelous shadows. Between outcroppings, or amid boulders, in front of fences, alone as a specimen, or used as a hedge, these evergreens are handsome and long-lived.

Where I grow some as a hedge, I use pine bark mulch around them, but they look extremely attractive when mulched with pebbles. I buy prepared evergreen fertilizer for them and feed them twice a season. Since their branches can withstand a very strong hosing, it is not contraindicated. As a matter of fact, it is the non-chemical way to get rid of insects.

   The low-growing, prostrate ones are excellent on an inclined rock garden. Upright ones look best in large rockeries, and the small rounded ones are excellent in a small rock garden. I used a low-growing *mugo* pine right in the center of my perennial border, and it looks just right. As specimens, they are perfect in a small "vest pocket garden," sentinels among clumps of *geranium* or *heuchera,* or by themselves.

spruce or hemlock   pine   thuga or chaemacyparis

   It is impossible to describe the fine differences in the needles and branching habits of the evergreens. Pines *(Pinus)* have long slender needles in clusters. Spruces *(Picea)* and hemlocks *(Tsuga)* have short needle-shaped leaves that grow perpendicularly along the branches. The spruce needles are more sharply pointed. The false cypress *(Chamaecyparis),* the arborvitae *(Thuga),* and the juniper have dense, fanlike leaves.

   Don't buy several all at once. There are many other dwarf evergreens you should learn about, such as firs and cedars and yews. This should only whet your appetite and introduce you to these marvelous and versatile plants.

   Whatever you decide to do, carefree is the word when you use plants for growing amid rocks. If you want to recreate a mountain scene in minia-ture, or a rocky glen, or a ragged hillside, be careful about proportion. Use conifers to tie in the area and large masses of small perennials for a rolling effect. Plan for sequential bloom in the rockery as elsewhere, and check for the sunlight requirements of each perennial. Just remember, before you dig a hole, make sure that Mother Nature is your landscaping partner.

   Many of the perennials listed in the glossary have dwarf hybrids which are suitable for rock gardening. Always check new catalogues for new varieties which may appear in the future. The following is a description of some plants not listed in the glossary which are, nonetheless, superb for rock gardens and available in most large nurseries. You may also want to try them in the border.

   Alyssum: Known as basket of gold, it is a prostrate, carpeting peren-nial with bright yellow flowers in spring and bright silvery green foliage. Does best in full sun and well-drained soil. Cut it back after bloom, particu-larly if it is growing out of a dry wall. Zones 3-8.

Arabis: Commonly known as white rock cress, *arabis* displays white blossoms about one-half-inch wide on foliage which rises about six inches from green rosettes. It needs sun or partial shade in good soil. It blooms in early spring, but some varieties bloom until June. It is a relative of *aubretia,* known as purple rock cress which, although lovely, is not as hardy, despite the claims of some nurseries. Try *arabis* instead. Zones 3-8.

Artemisia: This is a shrubby plant with many varieties suitable for the rock garden. Its chief attribute is the silvery, fernlike foliage. Good accent in ordinary soil in a sunny place. Zones 5-8.

Phlox: This is *phlox subulata,* not the tall border form. It is one of the prettiest and most carefree rock garden perennials. It forms a wide-spreading mat, which is solidly covered with tiny flowers all through May. It has furry foliage which remains evergreen through mild winters. Full sun is about all it needs to display its white, pink, or purple flowers. If it gets weedy, just tear some out. Garden experts may cringe at this advice, but it's all I do, and the flowers come back year after year. Zones 3-10.

Saponaria: Prostrate, compact plants with rosy flowers in May and early June. A few perennial varieties are hardy even up to Zone 2.

Thyme: This herb is lovely in the garden amid rocks, or on a wall. The densely matted tiny leaves are covered with rosy pink, miniscule flowers in June. It spreads easily, and like moss *phlox,* it is easy to control. It does better in full sun. Some varieties are hardy from Zones 3-10.

Tunica: Commonly called coat flower, *tunica* is covered all summer with small flowers resembling *gypsophila.* It grows to only a few inches in a sunny location. Soil should be well drained. It's hardy from Zones 3-10.

Perennials listed in the glossary which have varieties suitable for growing "on the rocks" include the following: *Achillea, astilbe, armeria, aquilegia, campanula, dianthus, dicentra,* heathers and heaths, *geraniums, gypsophila, heuchera, iberis, linum, lavandula, limonium, pentstemon, nepeta, primulas, salvia, veronica.*

Those of you living south of Zone 6 should try some of the saxifrages, low-growing, rosette-forming plants with many varieties of excellent rock garden plants.

Chapter 8

HERBALESSENCE

Anyone who raises teenagers, as well as plants, knows two things about them. One is that they are too busy listening to the radio to help with the gardening. The other is that they wash their hair almost daily. Their shampoos, as well as their cosmetics, are always "herbalessent." Guess what; you can grow many of these herbs right in your own garden.

If you like to cook — I don't — you can snip these ingredients right from a pot on your terrace, or from an herb bed near your kitchen, or from your perennial border. Some herbs, such as thyme, are also quite attractive. Many of them are annuals but are easy to grow. My husband grows enough tomatoes to feed Hartford, Connecticut for a month, so I grow annual basil for frozen tomato sauce. Dill, another annual, increases the therapeutic value of chicken soup, and parsley is actually pretty on a plate.

The following is a list of herbs that are hardy perennials. Grow these, and add them to soups, gravies, fish, lamb, chicken, beef, and veal. Buy them in collections, and create you own "herbalessence" garden.

Chives: Grows to two feet, with small purple flowers. Needs full sun.

Lemon balm: Two feet, partial shade.

Oregano: Two feet, shade or sun.

Peppermint: Two and one-half feet. Needs shade.

Rosemary: Two feet and up, not hardy below 0 degrees.

Sage: Three feet, blue florets. Needs sun.

Tarragon: One to two feet, pretty foliage, sun or shade. Not hardy too far below zero.

Thyme: In a sunny place, thyme is a lovely creeper with bright pink blossoms in June.

Shallots: Actually a bulb.

P.S. If you don't use these in the kitchen, how about blending them and adding them to your offsprings' shampoo?

Japanese iris *brings July color to a waterside garden.*

Chapter 9

COVERING SOME MORE GROUND

Groundcovers are traditionally recommended for
difficult areas on your property. Difficult usually means
too shaded, too steep to mow, poor soil, or whatever a
particular gardener finds to complain about. This particular gardener, as you know, finds work something
to complain about, anybody's work. I don't mow the
lawn; my husband does it, and watching him I've come
to believe that, unless you're hung up on miles of grass
that looks like broadloom, groundcovers are perfect for
every area you don't walk on. Once a low-care (Would
we consider anything else?) groundcover is installed,
it requires no maintenance. As if that weren't enough to induce you to try
it, some of the carefree groundcovers are also extremely attractive. There
are types for the shade and types that like only sun. Some like it hot, and
others are cool. Would you believe there are some that aren't happy unless
they are clinging to steep banks? I'll tell you about only the ones that are
really practically carefree.

polygonum

Before you choose any groundcover, you should know that the soil
must be prepared for these plants with great care, as it should be for any
perennial. Peat moss and 5-10-5 should be tilled into the ground. Unless
you are using one of the very rampant growers and spacing the plants very
close together, you will need to mulch the area the first season. Use finely
ground peat moss or small chips instead of nuggets which may be too big.
Mulching keeps the soil moist, which is a must for these perennials which
multiply by sending out runners. If the groundcovers are in the shade of
decidous trees, don't worry about the fall leaves. The shade-loving carpet
plants need the nutrition from the decaying leaves, and a strong hosing will
usually push the leaves to the ground between the plants. In the spring,
broadcast some dry 5-10-5, and water thoroughly. Don't use too many types
of groundcover. A more elegant, coordinated look is achieved by choosing
one or two types for shade, one type for sunny areas, and a creeping conifer
or vine for steep banks.

The following is a list of suggested groundcovers:

Ajuga: Commonly called bugle, *ajuga* is semi-evergreen, with oval

Lythrum, *known as loosestrife will bloom all summer in sun or partial shade.*

leaves that form a blanket quickly. It can grow in sun or shade, but the varieties with glossy, bronzy foliage do better in the sun. In May it throws spikes of sturdy blue, white, or pink flowers. It grows to about six inches, and when it spreads into the lawn, it can be mowed. Zones 5-10.

Cotoneaster mycrophylla: This hardy groundcover is a low-growing evergreen, which is actually a shrub. A dose of lime and a location in full sun are preferable. It flowers in May, and in the fall it displays bright berries which show until spring. It grows to about thirty inches but is prostrate.

Excellent for banks. Zones 4-9.

Epimedium: Green heart-shaped leaves of *epimedium* are leathery, and the stems, which are stiff, are covered with white, pink, red, or yellow blossoms. It produces clumps and spreads well in a peaty soil in partial shade. In the spring, the foliage has a pinkish hue. In the fall, the leaves turn reddish bronze. Zones 3-8.

Euonymus fortunei: This vine, know as wintercreeper, is a real troubleshooter. It does best in full sun or partial shade, and covers banks, inclines, and problem areas. The evergreen foliage turns purple in the fall. Zones 4-9.

Hedera helix: This is the familiar English ivy which is evergreen. It is a no-maintenace vine that quickly spreads and covers areas in deep shade. The foliage is ivy shaped and deep green. Zones 5-9.

Juniper varieties: The creeping junipers spread and maintain a height of about eight inches. Look for the words *procumbens* or *horizontalis.* There may be slightly taller varieties such as the Japanese junipers which are equally hardy and attractive. They like sun but manage very well in dry, sandy soil. They are a blue green, very versatile evergreen. Zones 2-9.

Pachysandra: This is the popular, foolproof, evergreen groundcover that does so well, even in dense shade. It will grow in the sun, too, but save the sunshine for the ones that prefer it. Pachysandra spreads quickly but can be contained with the mower. The flowers are not worthy of mention, but a hybrid with silvery white margins is. Zones 4-10.

Polygonum reynowtria: Polygonum, or fleeceflower as it is commonly known, is a wonderful groundcover for sunny places. It spreads rapidly with underground runners. It grows to about eighteen inches, has pale green foliage which turns bronze or red in the fall when it is capped with sprays of bright pink flowers. I love it and cannot praise it enough, but remember that it dies down in winter, so it may leave bare spots. Zones 4-8.

Vinca minor: This is the familiar periwinkle which is evergreen. It has dark green, leathery foliage which is capped with lavender blue flowers in May. Takes either sun or shade, but it does much better away from afternoon sun. Zones 5-9.

There are other excellent plants which may be used as groundcovers, but for large areas, the ones listed above are the best. In the section on gardening in the shade are references to wild ginger, *gaultheria, convallaria,* and *hosta,* which can also be used for carpeting but are versatile enough to be part of a border in the shade.

Two excellent carpeting plants are the bearberry and the rugosa shrub roses. See the section on gardening near the seashore where they are particularly suitable.

Purchasing groundcover for quick effects is very expensive, so choose with care. Remember, also, that the better the soil is prepared, the quicker and better they'll grow.

Dwarf evergreens, sempervivum, sedum *and* artemisia *turn an outcropping into a carefree rock garden.*

Chapter 10

THE STARS AND THE SUPPORTING CAST

What constitutes stardom in the perennial garden? Most gardeners would say beauty of bloom, length of flowering period, variety of color, and a long life. I would add that these top performers must also be easy to care for. My Oscars would go to the *peonies,* the *phlox,* the daylilies, and the hybrid *lilium.* To be sure, some of the supporting cast including the bit players are excellent, but these four are the indispensables.

When we bought our house, I didn't know the differences among most plants. I could identify *iris* and probably marigold. The former owner was not much of a flower lover, and as I mentioned earlier, the only perennials I found were some bearded *iris* and the *peonies.* In the spring the latter were heavy with fragrant, giant white flowers, spotted with pink. Although the grass and weeds were rampant about their crowns, they seemed unperturbed and bloomed for about two weeks, after which their foliage was lovely. I knew nothing of their culture and inquired

peony

about them. The former owner told me that they had been there when she bought the house nine years before, that she did nothing to take care of them, and that they always performed beautifully. A neighbor had given her the bearded *iris,* to which she was equally indifferent. By the next spring, the *iris,* only five years old, wilted, and when I tore it out, I found iris borer in the rhizomes and discarded the whole bunch. The *peony,* on the other hand, repeated the good show, and by then I knew that this perennial and I were blissfully compatible.

Peonies are available in single or double flowers, or in tree forms. Unlike the herbacious *peonies,* those whose stems and foliage die down in winter, the tree *peonies* keep a woody stem all year. They are breathtaking when in flower in late May and early June. There are early, mid, and late season varieties, so you can enjoy their bloom for a month. Although they may grow in half shade, full sun really brings out their best performance. The true perennial type, once established, requires very little maintenance, and they live forever. Lore abounds about *peonies* which are generations old. My own experience has been with the herbaceous types, not the tree *peonies* which are really shrubs. However, I include directions for planting and caring for the tree varieties, which I have gleaned from extensive reading about them.

The real trick in growing *peonies* is proper planting. The best time to plant is in the fall before the first frost. Buy them from a reliable nursery. They should be well-rooted, two-year-old plants with at least three "eyes" or pink buds protruding. Prepare the hole for them about one week before planting. Choose a site that drains well and is protected from strong winds. Give each plant about three feet. Dig each hole about one-and-a-half feet deep, and two feet wide. The subsoil should be replaced with the topsoil mixed with dehydrated cow manure, a helping of bone meal, and three handfuls of 5-10-5. Don't use peat moss, since it could make the soil a bit too acid. Soak the hole thoroughly a few days before planting. Get some-one to help you, and while one of you sets the plant so that the eyes are exactly one-and-a-half inches below soil level, the other can accommodate the roots firmly, making sure the plant will not sink into the soil. This depth is very important to the plant's success, so make sure you tamp the soil around the roots firmly. Water thoroughly. In the winter, after planting, give the *peony* some cover in the form of straw or evergreen boughs. The following spring, sprinkle some wood ashes from the fireplace, or a little bone meal and a dash of fertilizer around the base, and cultivate lightly before soaking completely. I always give them a prophylactic spraying of fungicide to prevent blight. This should be done when the young shoots start to poke through the ground. Staking is always necessary to keep the heavy flowers upright. I use a three-legged wire stake placed around the crown very early in spring. As the plant grows, I accommodate the foliage within the stakes. By blooming time they are already concealed, and the stems don't topple even in a heavy downpour.

Keep mulch off the crowns of *peonies,* and remove grass around them. In the fall, cut the foliage down to the ground, and destroy it. *Peonies* will reward you, year after year, with sensational flowers, either double or single, in shades of creamy white, pink, rose, and crimson.

If you order tree *peonies,* remember that when mature they grow to four feet and spread generously. The flowers of the tree *peony* are enormous, and crinkly and crepelike in texture. The foliage of the tree is more narrow and finely cut. As with the other types, tree *peonies* should be planted where they may be left unmolested for years and years. They don't need full sun, and, as a matter of fact, their flowers do better in some dappled afternoon shade.

When you dig a hole for the tree *peony,* make it about eighteen inches deep, and mix the subsoil and topsoil with leafmold or manure, a dash of bone meal, and a few handfuls of 5-10-5. Each root has a knobby, grafted section which should be placed about five inches below the soil. Press in the surrounding soil to eliminate air pockets. Water deeply, and apply mulch the way you would for any perennial. After planting, keep watch on the plant, and remove all dead wood with a pruning shear. The first winter, mulch lightly, but thereafter, no winter protection is needed. Remember to dispose only of the foliage since the woody stems remain all winter. In the spring, treat them with a fungicide, and give them a light dose of fertilizer.

Thomas Hogg is a lovely variety of hosta, one of the most versatile, shade-loving perennials.

As I said before, I have never grown tree *peonies,* but I have been
assured that they are not difficult to care for, so I am planning to try two
Japanese tree *peonies* next fall. The herbaceous ones give me no trouble
at all, and they reward me with pretty cut flowers in the spring. They may
be grown in a large perennial border, but I prefer a single line against a fence
or a wall. Mine share the spotlight with some dwarf evergreens and a few
clumps of Siberian *iris.* Along that border, I have several daylilies whose
foliage compliments the blooming *peonies.* A few weeks later, the *peony*
greenery returns the favor when the daylilies start to show off. Even if you
try only one in a sunny corner where you can see it in the spring, by following instructions for planting, you will continue to enjoy the flowers year
after year. And as I pointed out, they are so carefree. They never need
dividing, are resistant to most insects, and fungus can be prevented so easily.
If the ants that keep crawling around their buds bother you, just shake them
off, but rest assured that they don't bother the plant.

The *hemerocallis,* or daylily as it is well known,
has flowers that are stars for only one day. However,
one plant may produce dozens of tall scapes which will
produce flowers every day for over a month. The
foliage of *hemerocallis* creates an arching mound of
long, bladelike leaves, and when they are growing
together, no weed would dare to grow in between. A
border planted only with daylilies is probably the
easiest to tend to. All it needs is a little food culti-
vated into the soil in early spring, and the plants will

daylily

reward the nonworker with hundreds of flowers. Hybridizers have produced
so many new varieties with so many different periods of bloom, that a border
of daylilies may flower from early June until frost. They thrive in full sun or
half shade, in any kind of soil, and they look great alone or in the company
of any perennials. They come in creamy yellows, bright oranges, delicate
pinks, hot pinks, deep gold, chartreuse, apricot shades, and reds. As of this
writing, there are no blues, but so much work is being done by developers
that there may be blues and purples available soon. There are dwarf varieties,
but the handsome ones grow on scapes two to four feet tall. Although one
of their leafless stems may carry as many as six flowers, they never need
staking.

The best way to buy daylilies is in a collection chosen by a nursery for
a long period of bloom. In my main perennial border, I have two collections
of a dozen plants each, and they flower riotously from late June to the end
of September. When the bloom subsides, I just trim the stems down, and the
foliage remains pretty and verdant. In another border I used twelve of them
in yellow and gold, and they are a cheery sight from late June to early August.

They are seven years old now and so thick they don't even need mulching. I have not divided them, and the bloom has not diminished. The only time I separate their roots is when I want to propagate some of my favorites. This is a tough job, described in the section on maintenance, and one which should be done on a cool day in the fall. Although you can divide them in spring, the bloom is not as heavy.

When you plant daylilies, make sure that you fan out the roots and give them plenty of room. Always throw a handful of 5-10-5 and a handful of peat moss into the bottom. Cut the foliage down, if you plant them in the fall, to encourage the roots, but in subsequent seasons, don't eliminate the foliage since it serves as winter protection. Give them a good drenching at least once a week. Most of them are absolutely free of pests and fungus, but if your border becomes infested, also give them a mild spraying.

Hemerocallis looks lovely anywhere, and it is hardy from Zones 2-10. Although they are great in a one-star show, I also love them with a supporting cast of *platycodon, phlox,* tall *salvia,* hybrid lilies, and other daylilies. In a shady, naturalized garden, I like them irregularly placed with purple *lythrum* and dark blue *lobelia.* Some bit players that look lovely in the forefront of a *hemerocallis* clump are *catanache, campanula* and *nepeta.* Actually, I can't really think of any flowers that daylily doesn't look pretty with. It sounds like I'm sold on these plants, right? You bet. The only thing I should caution you about is their spread. Always give them two-foot diameters so they don't encroach on other plants.

Most perennials cannot compete with annuals in the color ranges. Those that can, the *delphinium,* the asters, and chrysanthemums are just too finicky and demanding, so they cannot find a home in my heart or in my garden. The great exceptions are the *phlox,* the leading ladies of the July to September gardens. Their large heads are really clusters of florets about an inch in diameter, in colors from snow white, shades of pink and salmon, lilac and purple, and bright reds to the palest sky blues. Only yellows are missing. Many varieties have central "eyes" in each floret which are darker or contrasting. *Phlox* are beautiful to regard from afar where they

phlox

appear like clouds of color, or from very near where each head is a fragrant mound of color. They flower over a long period, with certain varieties starting in early July and others at progressively later dates. Since their blooming period is so prolonged, at some time they are all flowering together, and the sight is breathtaking. As a matter of fact, so breathtaking that I couldn't imagine a perennial border in the sun without them, even though they require a little more maintenance.

They grow from two to four feet tall on leafy stems. In the spring, each plant should be thinned so only three or four stems are left. By doing so, you ensure stronger, more floriferous stems which will not require staking. Although they love sunbathing, I grow them very successfully in a garden that gets dappled shade after two in the afternoon. The best colors and hybrids are the strain named "Symons-Jeune," but some of the standard varieties still have favorites like "Starfire" and "White Admiral." Another excellent *phlox* is a white oldtimer, "Miss Lingard," which blooms for a long time starting in late June. *Phlox* is another excellent plant which may be bought in a collection. White Flower Farm's pink and white *phlox* collection is excellent.

Spring or fall planting is recommended. They are hardy in Zones 4-7. Plant them about eighteen inches apart so that air will circulate freely. In the spring, don't cheat on thinning. As I mentioned earlier, I found this hard to do in my desire for a lot of flowers, but believe me, it's like taking candy away from a child just before the meal. It's better for the kid and better for the plant. Try not to sprinkle any water on the foliage, even though *phlox* are big drinkers. Just soak the ground completely about once a week. Despite their drinking habits, *phlox* can withstand periods of drought remarkably well. The mold that grows on their foliage is really not the dangerous mildew, but it detracts from their appearance, so spray captan in the early spring, and use a fungicide every ten days thereafter. Cut off all the flower heads after they have bloomed, both to promote new flowers and to prevent seeding. If some seedlings do appear, tear them out since only the roots of the mother plant keep the hybrid colors, and seedlings will grow into dark magenta flowers which bear no similarity to their beautiful progenitors. Divide *phlox* every four years, cutting all new growth away from the old woody center which is discarded.

I let tall purple *phlox* compete with bright daylilies and yellow *heliopsis,* with "White Admiral" doing its own act nearby. Pink *phlox* and *platycodon* are also excellent costars. The only thing to avoid with red or purple *phlox* are fuchsia and salmon colors. Those look better when they can show off away from their siblings, nearly white *platycodon* and hybrid lilies.

In the rockery, don't forget that the highly recommended moss *phlox* is a comely second cousin that always deserves attention for a cameo role in Act I.

The hybrid *lilium* is another great star of the garden. It gets shouts of "encore!" to no avail, because when the performance is over, it's through for the year. But what a performance! And there are enough varieties for every act, including an overture and an epilogue. *Lilium* are bulbous

lilium vp

flowers which thrive in half shade, with the foliage of other perennials to shade the ground and keep it cool. I said cool, not wet, since moisture can ruin it. Make sure that the ground drains very well, and keep *lilium* away from moisture lovers. When you plant bulbs, put them in late, even after the first frost. Dig the hole about six inches deep, except where the nursery recommends otherwise and make sure the soil is liberally mixed with peat moss or leafmold. Many nurseries offer them pot grown in the spring, and I have purchased them quite late, even on sale, and had bloom that very summer.

When you receive the bulbs in the fall, put them into the ground right away. If you buy them pot grown, do not shake the soil loose as you would with other pot-grown perennials. They dislike being out of the ground even for short periods. If you opt for the newer hybrids, they are not prone to insects and disease, and regular spraying will take care of all their needs. Except for the ones that grow to only three feet, most of them require staking. I find the shorter ones just as splendid as the taller ones, so I try to stick to those, but don't neglect the "Imperial" strain  which grows very tall. A bamboo stick centrally located behind the stems will support them and remain concealed. After blooming, cut off all the flower heads, but leave most of the stem since the leaves contain the food-producing organs for the bulbs. Apparently the bulbs then store this food for next year's growth. Only when the stems have died in the late fall is it advisable to cut them down to soil level.

lilium

Lilium needs the same fertilizing and preventive spraying that the other perennials in the border get. Therefore, you can either grow a bunch of them together, or use them interspersed among other perennials for color accents. I have planted them among daylilies whose arching foliage keeps the soil around the *lilium* bulbs cool and weed-free.

If you study their bloom period, you can have these glorious flowers all summer long. Each one blooms for about two weeks, and a dozen varieties will have several bulbs flowering together. A very convenient way to order them is in collections which include many *lilium* forms. There are trumpets, bowls, pendant types, and those with petals curved back. Take a chance on them. I never saw one that wasn't beautiful, and most of them are show-stoppers.

I have never divided *lilium,* even after seven years of bloom, but I'm told that this form of propagation is simple and rewarding. Some forms produce little bulblets near the soil line around the stem, and others have tiny bulbs where the leaves emerge from the stalks. These may be planted for production of new plants. Another form of propagation is to lift the bulb out of the soil and detach and replant the scales which are attached to the base of the bulb. Other types of *lilium* bulbs actually produce new bulbs as offshoots, and these may be separated and replanted. All these forms of separation and replanting are supposed to produce new plants identical to the parent. I never did it, but I promise you one thing about these hybrid lilies. Although they are real aristocrats, they don't behave like prima donnas, and they get along with all the regular players in the cast.

These four stars are my favorites, but don't disregard the rest of the troupe. Siberian *iris,* which has a small role since it blooms for only about two weeks early in the season, is still a favorite of mine. The flowers are pretty, the foliage is lovely, and it takes care of itself forever. Some of the bit players, like *dianthus* and *heuchera,* will sometimes upstage the stars, because they flower all season in such bright shades of pink and red. The standbys like *heliopsis, valerian, lychnis,* and *monarda* have great dramatic moments of their own. *Lythrum, veronica, achillea, coreopsis,* and *salvia* are on stage all the time, with the *geranium, catanache, nepeta,* and *linum* trying to get your attention stage front. The first act brings you the talents of *thermopsis, aquilegia, digitalis, dictamnus,* and *trollius,* and the last act gives *aconitum, liatris, lobelia,* and *anemone* a chance to show off. Even a darkened stage will glow with *astilbe, primula,* and *convallaria,* not to mention the great set designs by *hosta* and ferns.

Remember that even the Sarah Bernhardts of the garden world have some periods of poor performance, so always reserve ad-libs and walk-ons for some of the supporting cast. And don't forget the great "rock" stars I told you about. All in all, it's a great show.

Chapter 11

SOMETHING A LITTLE SHADY

Nothing is more frustrating to the novice gardener than to try to figure out what shade really means. Before you remain in the dark, I'll tell you. Shade means away from the sun's rays for most of the day. It does not mean the absence of light, nor does it mean a dense, dark, woodland type of ambience. There are woodland ferns and wildflowers that will grow in those situations also. The shade I refer to occurs under the branches of deciduous

trees, where wind movement and shifting sunlight create a sunless brightness. Partial shade or partial sun means about five hours of sunshine and absence of direct sunlight for the rest of the day. Most perennials, even the sun-lovers, will succeed as long as they get about six hours of sunshine daily. There are some lovely plants that actually prosper away from direct sun for most of the day, but even those will not be hurt by some morning sunshine. What I'm trying to tell you, at the risk of increasing your confusion, is that you cannot be too rigid about this, and I'll even give you a list of plants and some ideas for heavy shade. Don't just throw in the trowel.

First, let's start with partial shade. For part of the afternoon, a nearby tree or a wall of a building causes shade to prevail. Although you can't prune a wall, you can certainly do some judicious cutting of several branches to permit more light to filter through. Before you attribute plant failure to the lack of sunlight, examine other causes. First of all, your soil must be well prepared as for any successful border. Water retention is even more important in shady areas. To begin with, your garden may be competing with the roots of the trees. Some trees are "waterholics" and drain the surrounding area of gallons of fluid daily. Secondly, the overhanging branches or the side of a building may be diminishing the amount of rainwater that actually reaches the soil. The garden in the shade needs extra humus and mulching so it can store the extra water it should receive. One thing in your favor is that evaporation is also reduced in the shade. Fertilizing and renewing the soil is something you should do, anyway, wherever your plants grow. Even if your main perennial border is in partial shade, you don't have to do without color and variety, and remember the advantages of being able to do your work without the sun beating on your back.

Perennials that don't mind part shade are *aconitum, anchusa, anemone, aquilegia, astilbe, baptisia, campanula, convallaria, dicentra, dictamnus, geranium, hemerocallis, heuchera, hosta, iberis, lobelia, lychnis, lythrum, monarda, oenothera, platycodon, primula, thalictrum, tradescantia, trollius, valerian* and *vinca.*

Among those listed are some that do very well even in areas that get more shade than sun. Again, I stress that strong light is not absent, just *direct* sunlight is. A naturalized garden, one that is irregular in the distribution of plants, that looks as if it were growing there without any plan at all, is the loveliest in the shade. Forms and foliage seem even more outstanding away from the sun. White is perfect in a shaded garden, and I try to use varieties of plants with white flowers. *Platycodon, astilbe, monarda* and *aquilegia* have excellent white flowers. *Convallaria,* the exquisite lily of the valley, has tiny, bell-like, white flowers which dangle amid erect, leathery green foliage. Some people like to use *convallaria* as a groundcover, but I prefer a small drift of it in the naturalized garden. Siberian *iris* has beautiful white flowers, and the *hosta* with the foliage that is variegated or banded with white is superb.

I am a stickler for attractive foliage in any garden, but the plants with the best foliage seem to be those that do well in the shade. *Platycodon* has dark green, finely cut leaves, the purple *lythrum* always retains sturdy stems smothered with bloom all season, and the mintlike foliage of *monarda* is always attractive. The multicolor *primulas* have rosettes or mounds that retain good form and color, *aquilegia* and *trollius* have deeply cut, ferny leaves, and *astilbes* have deep green or bronzed leaves. My favorite foliage plant is the *hosta.* These perennials are so versatile they can be used for groundcovers, for edging, as part of the flower border, in spreading clumps by themselves, or as companions for groundcovers. There are so many variations in leaf color, size, and shape, and so much confusion about their names, but they are all great, no-care plants. Some have white bands or margins and purple, bell-like flowers in August or September, held on tall stems high above the large ovalated leaves. Others have blue green, enormous leaves, with white flowers just above the crown. Leaf sizes vary, and although most of them are about a foot long, the width runs from two to eight inches. The *hostas* die down completely in the winter, leaving spots bare, but they come up in early spring and spread so quickly that weeds can't grow between them. Dividing them is very easy, and you can turn four plants into sixteen in a

A border of peonies *is at its glory in late spring,and the foliage creates a neat hedge after flowering.*

few years' time. Once you have a good planting of them, they need practically no care. Buy them in collections, and sit back and enjoy them.

The shady garden can also be a source of color from early spring through fall. In addition to those perennials with white varieties mentioned earlier, there are blue *aconitum,* multicolor *lilium,* yellow *trollius,* yellow and strawberry *digitalis,* multicolor *primulas* and *tradescantias,* cherry red *dicentras,* and pink *anemones.* Besides white, the *astilbe, iris, aquilegia, monarda,* and *platycodon* also come in bright colors.

Don't disregard a rock garden in the shade. Some of the low-growing, flowering perennials, ferns, and groundcovers can turn a boulder in the shade into a shrine away from the sun. Wild ginger, with the botanical name, *asarum europaeum,* originates in Europe and can be grown in Zones 4-8. It grows about five inches tall and has bright green, glossy, heart-shaped leaves. It loves shade, and a rock garden is ideal for it, although you may want to use it just as a groundcover for a small area. Another groundcover also suited for use in the rockery is *gaultheria procumbens,* known as wintergreen. By now you should know that *procumbens* means prostrate or creeping. Wintergreen is also evergreen. It has shiny, bright green leaves, about an inch long, drooping white flowers in May, and bright red berries in the fall. The berries are not poisonous, and when you crush the leaf, the fragrant aroma of wintergreen is very apparent. Try to use ginger and wintergreen in a corner or amid some large stones. They don't have the energy to cover large spots that some other groundcovers do, but for accents they are lovely.

I hesitated before to mention ferns. The reason I feel so ambivalent about them is that I prefer flowering plants. On the other hand, I did stress foliage, and ferns certainly have lovely foliage. However, they tend to look pretty much the same, given a few differences in form. But, they do grow in the shade and are not hard to naturalize. Still, you can find them almost anywhere, growing wild. You see what I mean? Oh well, I started, so I may as well tell you a bit about them.

Ferns have been growing on the earth for millions of years. Museum reproductions show mammoths plodding among them. I'm sure Adam and Eve found them in the garden of Eden and its environs. I'm equally sure that if you have any woods on or near your property, you have them growing there, and since it seems to be Mother Nature's pet child as well as her first born, perhaps you should get to know the fern.

Some ferns grow well in full sunlight, but all of them prefer the shade, and since that's where I've used them, I won't go into their use elsewhere. Also, since the vast majority love a woodsy, acid soil, I'll omit the ones that prefer alkaline soil. As usual, carefree is the guiding word, so I'm listing those ferns that will generally shift for themselves, whether you try them in the shaded border or in a rock garden. Most of them spread easily, so give them plenty of room or naturalize them, and you'll never have to divide them. Try these in a collection:

Christmas fern *(Polystichum bulbifera):* This neat grower can reach anywhere from fifteen to thirty inches. It stays evergreen until Christmas and is dark green with divided fronds.

Cinnamon fern *(Osmunda cinnmomea):* This one is tall and deciduous, growing from two to four feet. It needs a lot of moisture. In the summer, the first leaves wither and are found at the base of the plant. Hence the name.

Hay-scented fern *(Dennstaedtia punctilobula):* This one will spread and spread and grows to about twenty-four inches. It is pale green and feathery.

Japanese painted fern *(Athyrium goeringianum):* Grows to about a foot and a half. It has many shadings of green, including a silvery sheen. It is quite rare but lovely.

Lady fern *(Athyrium filix-femina):* This one is extremely easy to grow, but it is not rampant. It grows to about three feet with very feathery fronds. I've found mine in the woods, and except for the fact that they get discolored in early autumn, they are a very pleasant sight.

Maidenhair fern *(Adiantum pedatum):* This is a very light green, delicate-looking fern which grows to only about one foot, but it fans out.

Marginal shield fern *(Dryopteris marginalis):* An evergreen, this one grows to about two feet, but it will not spread. It is graceful and bluish green all year.

There are some ferns which will not grow much above a foot, which are excellent among rocks, stones, or boulders. The following are a good selection:

Common polypody *(Polypodium virginianum):* This little evergreen has leathery leaves. It grows to about ten inches, and in the woods, it will grow right on rocks which is why it is sometimes called the rock cap fern.

Toothed wood fern *(Dryopteris spinulosa):* Another evergreen fern which will grow to about eighteen inches. It has a lacy effect, and you'll often find it in florists' arrangements. I like it in the rock garden.

Rusty woodsia *(Woodsia ilvensis):* This fern grows best in the Northeastern regions. It grows to about six inches, has grayish green leaves and is perfect for the rock garden. Since it can take more light, try it near some *dicentra eximia* or some dwarf *astilbe,* and keep it wet.

As you can see, many plants thrive away from the sun. Under the branches of a tree, suspend a hanging fuchsia. One annual which I always

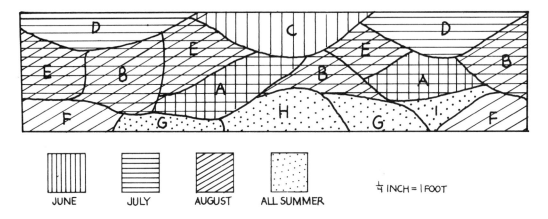

JUNE	JULY	AUGUST	ALL SUMMER	¼ INCH = 1 FOOT

ALL WHITE GARDEN IN THE SHADE

A)	*Astilbe*	24"	F)	*Hosta*	20"
B)	*Platycodon*	24"	G)	*Impatiens* (annual)	15"
C)	*Siberian iris*	30"	H)	*Heuchera*	18"
D)	*Japanese iris*	36"	I)	*Tradescantia*	24"
E)	*Monarda*	30"			

find a place for is the shade-loving impatiens, which has star-shaped flowers on glossy, inch-long leaves. The flowers come in pinks and reds, but my favorites are white. I can't imagine a more sensational flower than tuberous *begonias.* Try something a little shady, and remember, the secret is in the soil and maintenance, and of course, a lot depends on the gardener's sunny disposition.

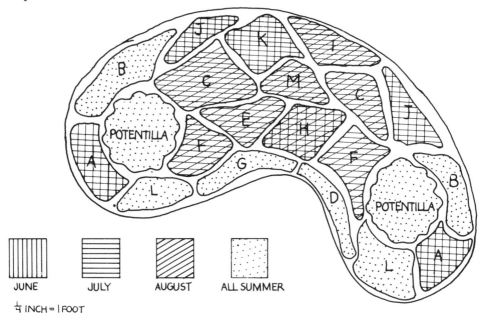

JUNE   JULY   AUGUST   ALL SUMMER

¼ INCH = I FOOT

GARDEN IN PART SHADE

	NAME	HEIGHT	COLOR
A)	*Astilbe*	18 - 30"	White, red, pink
B)	*Lythrum*	3 Ft.	Purple
C)	*Daylily*	3 Ft.	Yellow, peach, orange
D)	*Dicentra*	1 Ft.	Pink
E)	*Monarda*	2½ Ft.	Red
F)	*Platycodon*	2½ Ft.	Blue, pink, white
G)	*Geranium*	1 Ft.	Blue, scarlet
H)	*Dictamnus*	2½ Ft.	White, pink
I)	*Thalictrum*	3½ Ft.	Lavender
J)	*Japanese iris*	3½ Ft.	White, lavender
K)	*Digitalis*	3 - 4 Ft.	Yellow, pink
L)	*Tradescantia*	1½ - 2 Ft.	Red, blue, pink
M)	*Liatris*	2½ - 3 Ft.	White, purple

Chapter 12

MONSOONS, SIROCCOS, AND HALCYONS

Put away your atlas, I'm just being funny. There are plants for every situation, and what I mean is that the prevalence of too much moisture, or prolonged dry spells, or salt spray should not deter you.

Some of you have springs which keep the soil damp, or lovely streams running through the acreage, or ponds, or just a lot of wetlands. Don't despair. There are lovely plants that cannot get enough water, and you've got the natural setting for them. Again, I must warn you that I don't mean a section of your garden that becomes a bog in the spring thaw and then dries up. Those situations need raised beds or mechanical drainage in the form of pipes under the soil. I'm referring to the banks of streams and ponds, or even marshy areas, where the water runs through the soil but drains well. You can turn the excess moisture into an asset and create a naturalized garden which will delight you with color and several flower forms. Add plenty of peat moss and builders' sand to the surface, along with about two pounds of 5-10-5 per 100 square feet of garden area, until the muddy earth becomes friable. Here you should plant large drifts of those perennials which take care of themselves as long as you give them room. Most of them are not fussy about sun or shade, provided there is enough light.

Some of the finest perennials in the border have been developed as hybrids of those wildflowers seen growing untended along streams or wetlands. Although the hybrids are more versatile, they do tend to keep the

moisture requirements of the species, so when you plant a garden in very moist areas, you are really imitating Nature, which is the name of the game in all but the most formal gardens. There are a few perennials I have not listed in the glossary because I don't use them for a typical border, but they are very satisfactory for wet places. They are the following:

Cimicifuga racemosa: Known as bugbane or snakeroot, the *cimicifuga* is a tall, handsome plant that grows to about five feet in partial shade. It has glossy, leafy foliage and spikes of flowers about a foot long. Sometimes the white flower spikes grow to three or four feet. Once it is established, it multiplies and never needs division. It blooms in the fall, and one hybrid, *cimicifuga simplex,* grows to only about three feet. Zones 4-9.

Cypripedium: This is a hardy orchid, commonly known as lady's slipper. Varieties include one that grows to a foot, with yellow flowers in late May *(calceolus pubescens)* and a taller one *(reginae spectabile)* which displays purple flowers in June. Zones 3-9.

Gentiana: There are several varieties of gentian, a marsh-loving plant, and several opinions on its culture. While no one will argue about the beauty of the bright blue, tubular flowers, some people say they are too hard to grow. I say, try it in a boggy area where you add a good amount of leafmold or peat moss. One variety *(septemfida)* grows to only about one foot, and in August, it is studded with one-and-one-half inch flowers. Zones 4-8.

Iris cristata: This is the low-growing, crested *iris* that loves damp soil in partly shaded areas. It grows to about five inches, spreads to form large families, and flowers in May and June in shades of blue or lavender with a pale yellow or white crest. Zones 3-9.

Iris versicolor: This blue flag *iris* will grow two to three feet and flower in June and July. It's not fussy about anything and never needs dividing. Zones 3-8.

Iris pseudacorous: The yellow flag *iris* grows to about three feet, and in May and June it displays flat-topped, yellow blooms on sturdy stems. It loves neglect and, like its cousins, the crested and blue flag *irises,* it may not be for the perennial border, but they are all good choices for very moist areas. Zones 5-10.

Trillium: The American woodlily is a spring-blooming wildflower, available from several nurseries. It grows in whorls to about a foot or a little taller, and in the spring, it shows pointed white or pale pink flowers on short stems, right above the leaves. The prettiest is the *grandiflorum* variety, known as snow trillium. Give it shade and room. Zones 4-8.

In addition to the seven perennials mentioned here, there are quite a few in the glossary that also respond well to having damp socks most of the time. They are: *astilbe, dicentra, digitalis,* ferns, *hemerocallis, hosta,* Siberian *iris,* Japanese *iris, lythrum, liatris, monarda, primula, thalictrum, trollius, tradescantia* and *valerian.*

A small reflecting pool is the center of a low maintenance garden planted with digitalis, aquilegia *and* dianthus.

Now we've coped with the wet and wild situation, but how about the other problem? Will anything grow in hot, sunny beds which dry up quickly? Weekenders have the additional worry of missing one weekend and, therefore, should concentrate on those plants that will resist drought. Of course, you have mulched carefully, but even so, you want some of the trusty perennials that can fend for themselves even if you take a few weeks off. They are: *achillea, asclepias, catanache, coreopsis, dianthus, gypsophila, heliopsis, hemerocallis, heuchera, limonium, linum, lychnis, nepeta, oenothera, platycodon, phlox, salvia, veronica.*

Those who live near the seashore have three problems which could discourage gardening. They are salt spray, high winds, and sandy soil. The first quick solution is to limit oneself to container gardening or to annuals. Attractive potted plants look lovely anywhere so why not on decks and porches. All they need is protection from the wind. Another solution is to build a raised border for perennials, with good soil at least one foot deep. This is best in front of a wall, or with judicious placement of shrubs and trees nearby. Winter protection with salt hay or evergreen boughs is essential for gardens along the shore. In the spring, add plenty of manure and peat moss to refurbish the soil. If sandy soil and wind are effectively dealt with, the salt spray will not bother the following: *armeria, dianthus, coreopsis, catanache, gypsophila, hemerocallis, heuchera, limonium, linum, monarda, lychnis, veronica.*

If the border is completely protected from the spray, you can add *achillea, asclepias, heliopsis, sidalcea, thalictrum, tradescantia, valerian,* and the standard annuals.

There are some beautiful trees which grow very well along the seashore. The Russian olive has silvery, willowlike foliage, and it thrives in the salty wind. The pines, which seem to prefer rocky, sandy soils, present beautiful accents in seascapes. The most notable are the Japanese black pine and the Austrian pine, both tall trees (thirty to fifty feet) with dense growth. The Japanese pine has black bark and an irregular outline which is interesting in a windswept site.

Shrubs can be grown along the seashore, also, provided you buy tough, wind-resistant types. Among the cotoneasters and junipers, there are excellent, colorful varieties which add beauty, as well as protection, from wind. The cotoneaster, mentioned as a groundcover earlier, is also excellent for covering sandy slopes, and don't disregard the taller types with oblong, glossy leaves that are covered with bright red cherries in the fall.

Some shrubs are of particular interest to the gardener near the sea. Clethra and heaths and heathers are discussed in the chapter on shrubs. The following are also seaworthy:

Myrica Pensylvanica: This is a bayberry that grows from three to six feet with an equal spread. It has lovely foliage and remains impervious to sand, spray, or wind. Zones 2-8.

Arctostaphylos uva-ursi: Uva-ursi means bear grapes, and the common names of this beauty are bearberry and kinnikinnick. This evergreen grows to about one foot, spreads over rocky, sandy slopes, displays pale pink flowers in May and June and red berries in fall and winter. Zones 2-7.

Rugosa rose: Although I love roses, I do not recommend them anywhere in this book, except for this hardy shrub. Unlike its relatives, the *rugosa rose* tends to itself in dry, windy sites. It grows to about five feet, and after showing bright white or red flowers all summer, it bears fruit in the fall. A shortie named "Max Graf" attains a height of only two feet, but it is prostrate and can form a mat that carpets a slope all summer. It has pale pink flowers. Zones 4-9.

Wherever you live, don't disregard the lovely possibilities for gardening, and don't take it on all at once. Decide which type of garden you prefer, and then make everything else as easy as possible. If you have a pond, you may decide to make that your garden center and leave the rest to groundcovers and shrubs. If your "island in the sun" is where you prefer to expend your energies, again, leave the rest to the hardworking shrubs, even in the shade. Speaking of shade, you may like to spend your time there, so let the shrubs do their thing in the sun.

Chapter 13

SHRUBS THAT ARE PERENNIALLY USEFUL

Shrubs are bushy, woody plants that have several permanent stems instead of a main trunk. Their uses are infinite, and they are indispensable in landscaping. They are used for foundation plantings, for winter color, for protection, for privacy; to provide foliage, flowers, and fruit; to define boundaries; as groundcovers, and as accents. They come in different sizes and shapes, and their ornamental value is varied. Some remain green all year, while some bear showy flowers in spring or summer; some have brilliant foliage, while others have clusters of fruit. Would you believe there are some shrubs that do all or almost all of those things and are still easy to care for? There are tomes written about these worthy plants and deservedly so. Read all about them but not in this book. I'll just tell you about some that can be grown in the border or as companions for flowering perennials. Need I tell you that I'm eliminating all the ones that require special maintenance? I've also left out those that grow very tall and need stepladders for pruning. Another thing I'm hedging is getting into the ones that need too much in the way of clipping and shearing. Don't get me wrong. I love azaleas and lilacs and mountain laurels, but I just want to concern myself with a few shrubs that add color and form to the flower garden.

Abelia: This lovely shrub grows to about five feet. It is semi-evergreen and known as glossy *abelia* because of its small, shiny leaves. In midsummer it shows clusters of somewhat tubular, small, pink flowers. All it needs in the way of pruning is a little thinning in the early spring. Zones 5-9.

Caryopteris: Sometimes this plant is called blue spirea or bluebeard. In a sunny, dry spot in the garden, it will grow to about two feet and spread about the same amount. In August it shows bright blue, fringed flowers on stiff spires above silvery foliage. If the winter is severe, it will die down to the ground, but in early spring, new growth will show. If it doesn't die down in winter, prune back to new wood in the spring. It's a very dependable little shrub. Zones 5-9.

Clethra: This low-maintenance shrub is often called summersweet or pepper bush. Although the indispensable *Wyman's Gardening Encyclopedia* says that the *alnifolia* variety grows to nine feet, all the ones I've admired stay at around four feet. They have upright branches, very slightly arched, which show turrets of fragrant, pink flowers in August. Although these shrubs do their best in light shade and moist soil, they do well in any soil in full sunlight. In the early spring, just a shaping is all they need. Zones 3-9.

Daphne: There are two *daphnes* of garden value. The "Somerset" hybrid is taller, growing and spreading to about three feet. The flower clusters appear on top of graceful, upright stems in early spring and again, in the fall. Foliage is silvery green. The *daphne cneorum* is a very compact plant which forms a mound about a foot tall and two feet wide. The flowers practically smother the plant in spring, and in the fall a less spectacular rerun can be expected. Both hybrids are evergreen, and the terminal clusters of fragrant flowers are bright pink. They love light shade and a dry soil. No pruning is necessary, except for occasional dried-out branches. Don't move them. Give them a little winter protection where the temperature drops more than 5 below zero. Zones 5-9.

Heath and *Heather:* In an alphabetical list I should really call heather, *calluna* and heath, *erica*. *Wyman's* lists them that way, but several excellent and informative catalogues place them together under H, and so will I. In addition, their care is so similar, and they are so often used together·successfully. They are compact, low-growing shrubs which are evergreen, and if carefully chosen, they will bloom every month of the year in temperate zones. *Calluna* hybrids bloom from June to November, but some *erica* hybrids start to blossom in December and go right into early spring. There are tiny ones that don't grow above two inches, and taller ones that reach twenty-four inches at most. The florets grow like little fringes on wiry, feathery stems in colors ranging from white to rose to mauve to crimsons and purples.

heaths and heathers

Although many of the *callunas* are bushy and upright, many *ericas* are prostrate creepers. However, each one is a delight and very versatile. They look great in rock gardens, in borders as edging plants, and in "islands" with one another. The most beautiful border I ever saw is at White Flower Farm in Litchfield, Connecticut, but several reliable nurseries offer enough of both varieties to choose from. Some have controlled growth and others spread. They are all beautiful. With very rare exceptions they hate lime, so plant them in soil composed of woodsy, peaty soil, with plenty of sand. They love the sunshine and can withstand dry periods. Don't let them dry out, but don't keep them too moist. Naturalize them, and give them room. Remember, acid soil is really the only thing they demand. In the early spring, prune them back to new wood. They will not flower on last year's growth. In the winter, give them all a blanket of evergreen boughs or hay, even the ones that are hardy in Zone 3. Don't ever divide heaths or heather. You may propagate them by digging out a piece of root from the side. My advice is to enlarge your border by getting new plants. At first they look scrawny, but once an island or border is established, it is so easy to take care of and so rewarding. Use the small pine bark chips or finely ground peat moss for mulch. When you feed them in early spring, use 5-10-5, or even better, use evergreen fertilizer which is usually 7-7-7. Don't cultivate after feeding since the roots are so shallow. Just water deeply and thoroughly. Try them at the seashore. Zones 4-8.

Hypericum: These are lovely, low-growing shrubs that flower all summer. If you wish to use them as a low hedge, they are very cooperative and grow and spread into one another. As accents around the flower borders, they are excellent and provide golden yellow flowers which are about two inches wide and cup shaped. Even potted plants on sale at nurseries bloom like crazy. They grow from one foot to about two feet. One of the best varieties is *hidcote,* a twiggy type which will reach about eighteen inches. Some shorter hybrids may also be used as a groundcover. In the winter, if the tops die back as they do south of Zone 5, don't be dismayed because the spring will bring new growth. *Hypericum* is not one of the great shrubs, but it is reliable and pretty and really low care. Zones 4-10.

Philadelphus: This beautiful shrub is known as mockorange. It has pure white, fragrant, dogwood-like flowers which cover the branches in May and June. Although some grow tall, there is a dwarf named "Silver Showers" which grows to only three feet. All these fragrant shrubs are sensational when in bloom, and keep attractive foliage and a nice shape afterwards. Full sun or mid-afternoon shade are recommended. All it needs is a little shaping. Zones 5-10.

Potentilla: The shrubby *cinquefoli,* or buttercup shrubs as they are known, are very versatile and very pretty. They grow to about three or four feet, but light pruning keeps their shape and size to your specifications. The foliage is dark green, with small oval leaves. Insects and fungus ignore the *potentillas* which are covered with hundreds of rose-shaped blossoms in creamy white or bright yellow. The flower show starts in early June and goes on until frost. There is also a tiny dwarf which has bright pink flowers, and a creeper with minute yellow flowers. All of them like sun or part shade. Try them all as this is one plant to be enthusiastic about. Zones 2-10.

These shrubs are a mere handful, chosen because they can be part of the perennial border. Don't disregard the truly elegant shrubs like the *azaleas, rhododendron, kolwitzia, leucothoe, andromeda* and *viburnum.* Many of them will give you explosions of bloom and color in the spring. The *vibur-*

nums will delight you with berries in the fall. All the ones I mentioned can be cared for with just a bit of shaping and removal of dead twigs and branches. Find out about them, and pick two or three types, in addition to the coniferous evergreens I mentioned in the chapter on rock gardens.

Shrubs make an excellent background for the perennial border. Leave some space between the borders, though, so that neither the shrubs nor the perennials have to fight it out for food and water. The smaller plants like *potentilla* can be used as accents right in the flower beds, at the apex of a curve, in the middle of an island, or just growing amid your other flowers. Tall, blue plants like some *salvia, baptisia,* Siberian *iris,* or *aconite* look especially well as escorts to a few *potentillas.*

If you decide to use *potentilla* or *hypericum* as a hedge, let them go a bit, and don't make them too even and clipped looking. If you decide to create a hedge of heathers and heaths, buy them in a collection. You may purchase them for all year bloom, but I'm planning an "autumn island" of them to delight me after the pool is covered and the summer flowers are on their last stems (that's gardenese for last leg). I'd like to pull on a sweater and walk near the outcropping or rock garden as I know it, admire the dwarf evergreens, which are lovely in any season, and stroll over to the border of heathers and heaths which will be covered with flowers in purples, pinks, and whites. It makes me feel good just to think about it.

Chapter 14

BORDERLINE SEASONS

It's spring and the forsythia has bloomed. If you planted bulbs, they've come and gone, and the flowering trees and shrubs have been displaying their talents. The rock garden should be in its glory, spouting bouquets of *alyssum,* moss *phlox* and *arabis,* or multicolor *primulas.* The tufts of grasslike *armeria* are crowned by the bright pink or white caps of florets, and the candytuft is covered with white blossoms. In the border the *incarvillea* and the early *dicentra* compete with the golden blossoms of *trollius.* The *peonies* are pregnant with buds, and the *aquilegia* and Siberian *iris* are getting ready for their show.

spring iris

What have you been doing since early April? You've been working, because spring is the hardest time of all. You've renewed the mulch, given the borders and shrubs their first feeding, planted some new arrivals, renewed the soil, and sprayed fungicide on young shoots of bushy plants. You didn't forget to prune the heaths and heathers, but did you remember to thin and divide? When it rains you are inside tending to the potted plants you wintered indoors. When it doesn't rain, you are outdoors, watering the borders. Busy, busy, busy. Cheer up. The *iris,* the *peonies,* the *digitalis,* the *anchusa* and the *baptisia* are going to bloom any second now.

Around Memorial Day I'm always sorry that I started this whole gardening thing. All the work I've done, and the garden is still skimpy. What's more, even though I've sprayed and prayed, there is still evidence of fungus, and after all this rain, the bugs are getting impervious to the chemicals. I cut down all the affected foliage and I spray again. Suddenly, like magic, June comes and the bloom starts. The *aquilegia* dances on fernlike foliage, the Siberian *iris* pops into flowers, the *peonies* are sensational, the *linum* and the *geranium* show their dainty single blossoms, and the reliable *valerian* and *dictamnus* shoot up sprays of pink and white flowers. I do my Esther Williams backstroke so I can admire the bright pink and red feathers of *astilbe* and the bright orange *lychnis.* If you choose to make this the highlight of your season, add the tall, yellow *thermopsis* and June-blooming *lilium.*

coreopsis - June to frost

As July approaches, the white Carolina *phlox* combines nicely with the spikes of purple *lythrum,* the bright blue *salvia,* white or blue turrets of *veronica,* veils of pink *gypsophila,* blue and white bells of *campanula,* pink and white *heuchera,* blue and white *catanache,* lavender *nepeta,* pink, white, and red *dianthus,* and yellow and white *achillea.* As the *thermopsis, aquilegia, dictamnus, lychnis* and *astilbe* go into their final act in July, the others continue, and in early to mid-month, they are joined by *coreopsis,* white, red, and pink *monarda,* golden *oenothera,* daylilies, and *lilium.*

Late July brings the incredible display of *phlox* in almost every color but yellow. If you plant them according to their bloom sequence, every week or so right through August, a new plant bursts into bloom, and at some point when they are all in flower at the same time, they are eye-catching and breathtaking. In mid-August, blue *lobelia* and *aconitum* compete with sprays of white or purple *liatris.* If you grow *anemone vitifolia,* their creamy pink blooms should appear now and last well until frost. Last year I was starting to rake leaves from the border while the *achillea, heliopsis, coreopsis,* and *phlox* were still blooming.

platycodon - mid summer

All summer I attended to some minor weeding, spraying insecticide and fungicide, and keeping the border neat. At most it took an hour a week. If you do the soil and spring routine correctly, and if you mulch, it should not take you any longer. In the fall, there are a few chores to do. When the first frost hits the potted annuals, it's time to discard them, and wash and store the containers. The fuchsia, lantana, and *agapanthus* should be indoors before frost, but dig up the dahlia tubers, and store them after the cold knocks down the foliage. Divide and transplant some of the rampant growers, and remember to cut down the foliage of all perennials except the heaths and heathers, the *caryopteris,* the *potentilla,* and the other shrubs. By now you've gotten your hands dirty (that's gardenese for getting your feet wet), and you'll be planning additions and changes for the border.

I'm sure that in the fall you will add *peonies, lilium* or other perennials. When December comes, give all new plants and recently separated and transplanted perennials some winter cover. I don't make much of winter protection the second year, except where directions call for it, or where I've strayed a bit in the hardiness zones. Pray for a good mulch of snow, but don't overdo it the way I did the winter of 1976-77. Buy yourself a few good books, including gardening books, and dream a bit. As the poet said, "If winter comes, can spring be far behind?"

Monarda *is known as bee balm because the exotic blossoms in bright pink, crimson, or white seem to attract bees. I call it gardener balm. It's so easy to grow and has a long flowering period.*

Dictamnus *is a long-lived perennial with turrets of pink or white flowers in June and July. It never fails to reward even the laziest gardener.*

Chapter 15

BORDERWISE

The following are some lists that will help you in choosing perennials for your borders. Remember that new hybrids are emerging all the time with new colors, heights, and periods of bloom. Always check recent catalogues before ordering.

summer *phlox*

Frontliners: dwarf to eighteen inches

alyssum, anchusa, aquilegia, armeria, astilbe, campanula, catanache, dianthus, dicentra, geranium, gypsophila, heaths, heathers, *heuchera, linum, limonium, lavandula, nepeta, oenothera, potentilla, pentstemon, primula, salvia, tradescantia, veronica*

Midliners: eighteen to thirty inches

achillea, aconitum, aquilegia, asclepias, astilbe, campanula, coreopsis, dictamnus, gypsophila, heather, heath, *hemerocallis, hosta,* Siberian *iris,* Japanese *iris, lavandula, liatris, lychnis, lythrum, monarda, peony, phlox, platycodon, salvia, sidalcea, tradescantia, trollius, valerian, veronica*

Backliners: thirty inches and up

aconitum, anchusa, baptisia, campanula, heliopsis, hemerocallis, Siberian and Japanese *iris, liatris, lilium, lythrum, phlox, potentilla, salvia, thalictrum, thermopsis*

White flowers

achillea, aquilegia, armeria, astilbe, campanula, catanache, convallaria, dianthus, dictamnus, heuchera, hosta, iberis, Siberian and Japanese *iris, liatris, linum, monarda, platycodon, primula, tradescantia, valerian, veronica*

Blue flowers

aconitum, anchusa, aquilegia, baptisia, campanula, catanache, caryopteris, hosta, Siberian and Japanese *iris, linum, monarda, pentstemon, platycodon, primula, phlox, salvia, tradescantia, veronica*

Lavender and purple flowers

aquilegia, campanula, Siberian *iris, geranium,* heathers, heaths, *hosta, lavandula, liatris, lythrum, limonium, lobelia, nepeta, pentstemon, phlox, primula, tradescantia, thalictrum, salvia, veronica*

Yellow flowers

achillea, aquilegia, alyssum, coreopsis, digitalis, heliopsis, hemerocallis, hypericum, linum, oenothera, primula, potentilla, sedum, thermopsis, trollius

Peach, orange, salmon flowers

asclepias, astilbe, hemerocallis, lilium, lychnis, pentstemon, potentilla, trollius

Pink, rose flowers

aquilegia, armeria, astilbe, anemone, dianthus, dicentra, dictamnus, geranium, gypsophila, heuchera, hemerocallis, incarvillea, Japanese *iris, lythrum, limonium, monarda, potentilla, primula, platycodon, pentstemon, peony, phlox,* moss *phlox, sidalcea,* thyme, *tradescantia, valerian, veronica*

True reds

astilbe, dianthus, achillea, hemerocallis, lilium, phlox, peony, tradescantia

Perennials that never need dividing

aconitum, baptisia, anemone vitifolia, asclepias, catanache, cimicifuga, dicentra, dictamnus, geranium, gypsophila, Siberian *iris, limonium, linum, lavandula, lychnis, nepeta, oenothera, peony, platycodon, salvia, thalictrum, thermopsis, veronica*
Shrubs do not need dividing, so add heaths, heathers, *hypericum, potentilla.*

Hardly ever need dividing so give them room

campanula, digitalis, hemerocallis, iberis, incarvillea, liatris, lilium, lythrum, tradescantia, trollius, valerian

Good for naturalizing

asclepias, astilbe, anemone vitifolia, cimicifuga, coreopsis, geranium, hemerocallis, all types of *iris, iberis, liatris, lythrum, lilium, monarda, thalictrum, tradescantia, trillium*

Perennials that grow well in pockets

anchusa, aconitum, baptisia, hemerocallis, heuchera, hosta, Siberian or Japanese *iris, liatris, lythrum, peony, lilium, thermopsis, tradescantia*

This garden is deceptive. Although it looks very "landscaped," phlox, *daylilies and* hosta *are some of the most carefree plants in gardendom.*

Sequence of Bloom

Please note that this calendar chart is *approximate* and may vary in some zones. Some perennials have hybrids that bloom all season (Hurrah!) These are listed separately. Others have varieties with different flowering periods, and they will be listed accordingly.

April - May

alyssum, arabis, armeria, geranium, heaths, *iberis,* moss *phlox, primulas*

May - June

anchusa, aquilegia, geranium, heath, *incarvillea, iris* (Siberian, *cristata, versicolor, pseudacorous) peony, primula, trollius, veronica*

June - July

anchusa, aquilegia, astilbe, baptisia, campanula, dianthus, dictamnus, digitalis, geranium, lychnis, nepeta, pentstemon, primula, salvia, thermopsis, veronica, and varieties of *hemerocallis* and *lilium*

July - August

asclepias, campanula, catanache, coreopsis, dianthus, gypsophila, hemerocallis, hosta, lavandula, liatris, limonium, lilium, Japanese *iris, monarda, platycodon, phlox, sidalcea, salvia, thalictrum, veronica*

August - September

aconitum, anemone vitifolia, heather, heath, *liatris, lobelia, phlox, salvia, veronica*

Perennials with Long-blooming Hybrids

anchusa: June to September
achillea: June to frost
campanula: June to September
coreopsis: June to frost
dicentra: June to September (eximia hybrids)
geranium: June to September
gypsophila: late June to frost
heaths and *heathers:* early spring through winter
heliopsis: July to frost
heuchera: June to frost
linum: June to late August
lythrum: June to September
nepeta: June to September
oenothera: late June to September
pentstemon: late June to late August
phlox: July to frost; Carolina *phlox:* late June to August
salvia: June to August (May night); July to September (other varieties)
thalictrum: June to September
tradescantia: June to September
valerian: June to September
veronica: June to September

And don't forget *potentilla* and *hypericum* which bloom all summer long.

Chapter 16

SUMMING UP

I can just hear it now. "How dare she call herself a gardener? She left out poppies, and *delphiniums,* and *clematis,* and asters, and chrysanthemums." Or, "That woman should eat hemlock. Not one word about bulbs or bearded *iris."*

lilium

I'll neither eat hemlock nor my words. I told you in the beginning that this book is for the novice who does the work himself and gets turned off by books that teach him more than he wants to know. It's for those who want flowers, lots of them, without making a life's career out of it.

If you want to learn more and do more, there are some marvelous books to read. I'll even give you a partial list of catalogues and books to look for. I just wanted *this* book to leave you with a yearning to grow some flowers and to give you the assurance that you can do it. Perhaps you'll find too little here, and gardening will become the endlessly rewarding and fascinating hobby it can be. Or, you may decide to try just a dozen plants for some summer color. Either way, you'll enjoy yourself. I do.

Bulbs have been left out because any salesperson in a nursery can give you directions for planting and caring for them. They require good drainage and good soils the way any other plants do. From time to time, I plant a few dozen tulips, but once the flowers are spent, I have to leave the brown and wilted foliage or spoil next season's bloom. *Narcissus* are pretty, nodding their lovely heads in the spring, and they form large colonies without the necessity of renewing. If bulbs entice you, by all means, plant an acre of them, but I can't see getting hunchbacked just for a week's show in the spring. That's not my style.

As to some other plants you might find missing, read all about them, and you'll find they act just like aristocrats. They need support, they have to be divided frequently, or they are very hospitable to bugs and disease. I think there are enough carefree plants to choose from.

All the perennials listed in this book, including dwarf evergreens, shrubs, groundcovers, and plants for special conditions are the ones I've had exper-

ience with and found easy to care for. The glossary should give you enough
of a choice for more than one border, but if you still want to try your thumb
with some of the aristocrats, go ahead. Just don't say I didn't warn you.
You can be a lazy gardener, but not a neglectful gardener, so follow directions
carefully. You may have some failures, but most of the time, you'll have
lovely flowers.

Remember, I never promised you a rose garden.

GLOSSARY

Abelia: Lovely shrub. See chapter 13.

Achillea (yarrow): Very useful border perennial with a very long blooming period. Flowers appear in clusters on top of wiry, fernlike foliage. Heights vary from a tiny white dwarf with single flowers to thirty inches in the yellow or red varieties. An excellent white *achillea* is the "Pearl" with perky, single blossoms atop eighteen inches of bright green foliage. They withstand dry spells and thrive in ordinary garden soil in a sunny area. They bloom from June to frost. Divide every three or four years. Zones 3-8.

Aconitum (monkshood): Like their common name, *aconitum* flowers resemble bright blue helmets which appear laterally on tall, sturdy stems above dark green foliage. Heights range from three to five feet. All varieties prefer moisture in a shady area. Don't ever move or divide them. They flower from mid- to late August until frost. Zones 3-7.

Agapanthus (lily of the Nile): See chapter 6.

Ajuga (bugle): Great groundcover. See chapter 9.

Alyssum (basket of gold): Lovely edging plant or rock garden perennial. Spring blooming. See chapter 7.

Anchusa (alkanet): Most of these bright blue, single flowers show in spring through early summer on stems that grow from eighteen inches to four feet. The best type for the perennial border is the tall "Royal Blue" variety that flowers most of the summer. A dwarf with brilliant blue flowers is pretty in the rock garden in early summer. All *anchusas* prefer light shade or sun in well-drained soil, and all of them have good foliage after bloom. Divide every three years. Zones 3-8.

achillea   aconitum   anchusa

Anemone: Only the grape-leaf *anemone,* the *vitifolia,* is recommended. It blooms in mid-August, and if mature, will flower until frost. The flowers are creamy pink, about two to three inches wide, on sturdy stems about thirty-six inches tall. They love the cold and multiply readily in very woodsy soil containing leafmold. They prefer shade and never need dividing. Zones 4-8.

Aquilegia (columbine):   These are delightful, dancing flowers which bloom in late May through most of June, on stems that grow from ten inches to thirty inches, depending on varieties. They like good soil in light shade. There are lovely white, yellow, and blue columbines, but the prettiest are those with petals and corollas in contrasting colors. "Rose Queen" has petals in bright pink with creamy white centers. After bloom, trim the foliage so that it doesn't flop over. If kept free of insects, the leaves will not mottle and turn brown. *Aquilegia* is not long-lived, and after a few

anemone   aquilegia   armeria

years in the border, the bloom will diminish. Don't divide; it doesn't help; go get new ones. They are all beautiful. Zones 3-8.

Arabis (rock cress):   Lovely edging or rock garden perennial. See chapter 7.

Arctostaphylos uva ursi (bearberry):   Great groundcover for sandy slopes near the seashore. See chapter 12.

Armeria (sea thrift):   Tiny white or pink globular flower clusters appear above grassy tufts of foliage. If you cut the five-inch stems down to the grassy mounds, you may get another round of blossoms, even after the flowering period in May and June. This perennial loves a hot, dry, sunny spot in a rock garden or in an edging border. To divide, just lift the shallow roots and discard the wasted center. Zones 3-8.

Artemisia: Shrubby foliage plant with some interest for border but best in the rock garden. See chapter 7.

Asarum: Wild ginger. Beautiful heart-shaped leaves in a bright green. Lovely in a rock garden in the shade, or as a groundcover for a small area. See chapter 11.

Asclepias (butterfly weed or swamp butterfly):   Why should this pretty plant be called a weed. The clusters of bright orange florets show most of the summer on foliage about two feet high. It loves the sun but fares equally well in dry or very moist soil. Never needs dividing. It's hardly a star but definitely not a weed. Zones 3-9.

Astilbe (false spireas):   These are some of my favorite perennials. They have deeply cut, glossy foliage. Even when the bloom subsides in August, the leaves turn a bronzy color and remain elegant. They love a moist, shady place, but they are impervious to morning sun. The flowers look like feathers in shades of white, pink, salmon, and bright red. They range from a dwarf to two-and-a-half feet tall. They are big drinkers and big feeders, so give them room. Their colorful plumes never fail to please. Buy them in collections, and propagate when you divide them every four years or so. Zones 4-8.

Baptisia (indigo):   A tall, shade lover which blooms from late May until mid-June. The flowers are small, pealike, bright blue, and they grow along stems that rise to about three-and-a-half feet. The foliage is clover-like and pretty after bloom when the spikes display fat seed pods. *Baptisia* does well in sun or light shade in ordinary soil. Never needs dividing, but give it about one-and-a-half feet centers in the back of a naturalized border. Zones 3-10

asclepias   baptisia   astilbe

Campanula (bellflower):   There are dozens of groupings listed in gardening books, but for our purposes, the following will suffice: a) *carpatica;* b) *rotundifolia;* c) *persicofolia.* The *carpaticas* are a dwarf group which grows to about eight inches. The bright blue or white little bells wave on wiry stems above tufted foliage all summer long. The *rotundifolia,* known as the bluebells of Scotland grow from fifteen to eighteen inches. Somewhat pendulous, they dangle dainty blue or white flowers from July until frost. The *persicofolia,* known as the peach-leaved bellflower, is taller and grows to about two-and-a-half feet. The flowers which appear in early June last until mid-July. They are lavender blue or clear white. All the *campanula* do well in good soil, in a sunny or partly shaded border or rock garden. The smaller *carpatica* and the *rotundifolia* may go for five years without dividing. The taller *persicofolia* may need dividing every third year. Plant them only in the spring. Zones 3-10.

campanula   catanache   convallaria

Caryopteris (blue spirea):   Sturdy shrub, small enough for the border when an autumn blue is needed. See chapter 13.

Catanache (Cupid's dart):   Lovely blue or white cornflowerlike blooms appear in July and August. The foliage is thin and woolly, and the flower petals are stiff with serrated edges. They grow to about eighteen inches, but there are new hybrids that are taller. All they seem to require is sunny, dry soil in the front of the border. Dry them by gradually removing water and hanging them upside down in a dark place. They never need dividing. Zones 5-10.

Cimicifuga (snakeroot): Tall perennial that is great for the banks of rivers and ponds, or in a wild garden in part shade. See chapter 12.

Clethra (sweet pepperbush):   Lovely low-care shrub that looks good in the background of perennial borders. See chapter 13.

Convallaria (lily of the valley): This is an old and well-known garden plant with many uses. It has firm, upright, ovalated, dark green leaves which are about eight inches tall and two inches wide. The blossoms, which appear in late May, are white, bell-like, tiny, and fragrant. *Convallaria* likes a partly shaded location where it can spread and spread and spread. Give it a thick, woodsy soil, and plenty of water. Divide it to propagate, and find little "pocket gardens" for it. Just give it an annual feeding. Zones 2-8.

Coreopsis (tickseed): This is one of the most reliable plants in the border. Bright yellow, daisylike flowers grow on thin, leafy, wiry stems. Although some varieties grow to thirty inches, the stalks tend to droop. A shortie named "Goldfink" has stems about ten inches tall, and like its brothers, it will bloom all summer. Bugs and disease seem to disregard *coreopsis*. Just let it bask in a sunny place. Mine disappear after three years, so I just replace them, but my neighbors claim they can last longer and should be divided every three years. Zones 3-10.

Cotoneaster (rock spray): A great groundcover with lovely red berries in the fall. See chapter 9.

Cypripedium (lady's slipper): Exotic wildflower for wet areas. See chapter 12.

Daphne: Lovely shrub with evergreen foliage and gorgeous clusters of flowers. Small enough for a border. See chapter 13.

Dahlia: Lovely tuberous plant for containers. See chapter 6.

Dianthus (pinks): These are excellent rock garden or edging plants for the border. There are dozens of annual, biennial, and perennial varieties. For our purposes, the perennial *dianthus alwoodii* is the best and comes in dozens of shades of pinks and reds. They grow from mounds on stems about ten inches tall, and they will keep blooming from June to frost, if you cut back spent blossoms. Give them water, lots of sun, and a sprinkling of lime. If you choose to propagate them, the roots are shallow and practically fall into divisions. However, they are slow to spread so buy yourself a whole bunch. Zones 3-10.

coreopsis

dianthus

Aquilegia *is one of the highlights of the early June garden.*

Dicentra (bleeding hearts):   The tiny, rosy red flowers are heart shaped; hence its name.   The *dicentra spectabilis* is tall and has lovely flowers on arching branches.   However, it disappears in the summer, so look for the *dicentra eximia,* or plumy types.   They are not as tall, but their foliage is feathery and deeply cut, and they flower from late May until frost. Give them a place in part or mostly shade, lots of moisture, and lots of room.   They don't spread rampantly, but other plants do, and *dicentras* resent being moved or divided.   Zones 3-7.

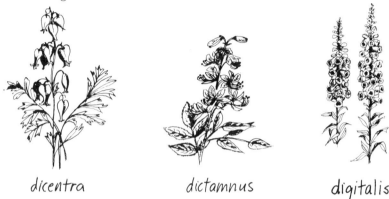

dicentra   dictamnus   digitalis

Dictamnus (gas plant):   This lovely mid-border perennial cannot be praised too much.   It's not the least bit demanding about soil, likes the sun, but will thrive away from it too.   The foliage is a lime green color and shrub-like.   The small, oval leaves cover the plant, and in June and July, spikes grow to about thirty inches and are covered with small pink or white flowers.   It takes a while for a *dictamnus* to settle into its home, but after a few years, it will throw dozens of flower-laden spires.   Gas plant is long-lived and cannot tolerate moving or dividing, so give it about a foot and a half.   Zones 2-8.

Digitalis (foxglove):   Even if the drug for cardiac patients were not derived from this plant, it would do your heart good to see a massing of foxgloves in bloom.   Most varieties are biennial, but two excellent perennials are the *ambigua* with yellow flowers, and the *mertonensis,* with rose-colored flowers.   The yellow foxglove grows to about three feet, and the flowers are tubular and face down.   The *mertonensis* can reach five feet, but the stems are sturdy, and the flowers face outward.   They both bloom in June and July in a shady, moist area.   Mine have died after three or four years, so I usually replace them, but some gardeners claim they can be divided. Try them anyway.   Zones 4-10, but in the north, only spring planting.

Epimedium: Lovely groundcover for partial shade.   See chapter 9.

Euonymous: A no-care, shrubby groundcover. See chapter 9.

Ferns: Good foliage for naturalizing in the shade or in very wet areas. See chapter 11.

Evergreens: A must for all gardens; the dwarf conifers are the best rock-garden plantings I know of. See chapter 7.

Fuchsia: Exotic container plant which can be wintered indoors. See chapter 6.

Gaultheria (wintergreen): Aromatic leaves, pretty flowers, and bright red cherries. Lovely for rock gardens in the shade. See chapter 11.

Gentiana: Bright blue flowers, good for swampy area. Chapter 12.

Geranium (cranesbill): Don't confuse these with the pelargonium, the tall, summer flowers in white, red, and pink. These *geraniums* have dainty, single blooms on finely cut leaves. The flowers are about one-and-a-half inches wide, and they come in shades of pink, blue, lilac, and crimson red. Some are really tiny, up to six inches, and bloom in May and June. The *dalmaticum* are white or pink dwarves which bloom all summer. The *sanguineum* are reddish purple, about ten inches tall, and they bloom from May until mid-August. "Johnson's Blue" and "Wargrave's Pink" are about one-and-a-half feet tall and show flowers from June to late August. Sun or part shade, any soil, and don't divide them. Although they look delicate, they are truly hardy. Zones 4-8.

Gypsophila (baby's breath): The tiny flowers of *gypsophila* barely measure one-quarter inch. They are white or dainty pink, and they flutter on wiry, veil-like stems. You've seen them often in winter bouquets. The taller ones bloom in June and July and spread about three feet. However, wind topples them so they have to be staked. I prefer the tiny creeper for the rock garden and the eighteen inch "Rosy Veil" or "Pink Fairy" for the border. Their stems topple a bit also, but they form mounds of woolly foliage covered with dainty, pink flowers, which bloom all summer, even to frost. Give them a sprinkling of lime, lots of sun, and lots of water, and never move any *gypsophila;* they also need room. Zones 3-8.

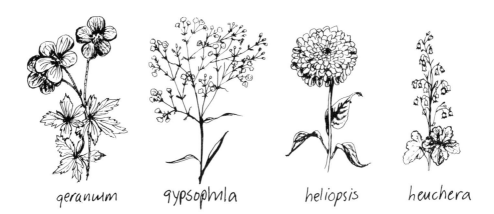

geranium   gypsophila   heliopsis   heuchera

Heaths and Heathers: Lovely shrubs with so many uses in the border, in the rock garden, or on their own. See chapter 13.

Hedera (ivy):   A lovely vinelike groundcover for shady slopes. See chaper 9.

Heliopsis (false sunflower):   This is a rugged, tall perennial for the back of the border. It has sturdy stems that don't need staking, deeply lobed, bright green leaves, and bright, cheerful yellow flowers with many petals, about three inches wide. They start blooming in July, and the more you cut, the more they bloom. Dry the flowers by hanging them upside down in a dark attic or cellar. They love the sun and rich soil, but they can take care of themselves. I love them with dark blue flowers or purple *phlox.* Divide new roots from the woody center every four years or so. Zones 3-9.

Hemerocallis (daylily): One of the greatest border plants. It is certainly the most carefree perennial I know of. See chapter 10.

Herbs: Many can be grown in pots or in the flower bed. See chapter 8.

Heuchera (coral bells):   This beauty is also known as alum root. I call it the best edging plant in gardendom. With just a little sun or light shade, a dose of food, and a drink of water, this lovely perennial blooms all summer long. The stems grow out of rosettes of ivylike foliage, and the flowers are like tiny bells, about one-half inch in size, which dangle in bright shades of pink and red and clear white. They rise about one to two feet, and from a few feet away, they look like bright sprays of color. In the rock garden or in the flower bed they are sturdy and withstand drought. Divide them every four years. Zones 3-9.

Hosta: Known as funkia or plantain lily. This is the most beautiful foliage
plant there is. It produces large mounds of oblong leaves that are deeply
lobed, twisted, or fluffy, depending on the variety. The "Thomas Hogg"
shows dark green leaves with a narrow white margin. Others have variegated colors mixing creamy beige, white, and green all in one leaf. In the
shade, the foliage is a refreshing sight, and the colors remain stronger,
although *hosta* also grows in the sun. It is compatible with *vinca* or
pachysandra, adaptable to a shady section of the border, and stunning as
a hedge by itself. Feed it, water it, and watch it spread. Divide every
three years, and watch it multiply. Most of the flowers are insignificant
and grow on tall scapes in blues or white. Nothing to rave about flower-
wise but a superb plant anyway. Zones 3-9.

Hypericum (St. John's wort):   Lovely little shrub with pretty yellow flowers
all season long. Good for edging, hedging, or border. See chapter 13.

hosta   iberis   incarvillea

Iberis (candytuft):   I prefer the common name for this lovely edging perennial. It is an evergreen which grows to about nine inches and forms large,
dense mats in sun or partial shade. The white flowers cap the thin, glossy
leaves from mid-May until early June. Some hybrids flower again in
September. If a particularly cold winter beats them up a bit, just shear off
the tops, and it will grow foliage and bloom. Like lily of the valley, the
perennial, candytuft, can be used as a groundcover or as an attractive mat
around a rock garden or a naturalized border. Give it room and you'll
never have to divide it. Zones 3-10.

Incarvillea (hardy gloxinia):   The *incarvillea* has bright pink clusters of
flowers, each of which is about three inches big. They grow on tall, leafless stems about one-and-a-half feet above glossy, oval leaves. They flower
in late May with bloom recurring through June. I give them winter protection in Connecticut. They are pretty and never need dividing which is
always a bonus. They like sun and a peaty soil. Zones 6-10.

Phlox *and* platycodon *are lovely compatible perennials for the midsummer garden.*

Iris: Three types of *iris* are very useful for naturalizing, or for wild gardens in boggy areas, or on the banks of streams, swamps, and ponds. They are the *iris cristata, verisolor,* and *pseudacorous* I described in chapter 12. For the flower borders, I prefer the Siberian *iris* and the Japanese *iris*. The Siberian is a rugged plant which grows in sun or shade and virtually takes care of it'self. Unlike its bearded cousins, it never needs dividing, is less prone to disease, and since the hirsute fellows bloom at the same time and for about the same period, I'd rather deal with the shaven Siberians. Their foliage is tall, thin, and bladelike. There are beauties in white, blue, lavender, and purple. My favorite is the "White Swirl" which has creamy flowers edged in yellow. I grow them with "Dreaming Spires" with lavender and royal blue petals. This fall, I will try a new dwarf from White Flower Farm, named "Flight of Butterflies." Not only are they exquisite in flower beds, but a clump of them near a garage, or in front of a shrub, or anywhere is a real delight. They grow to about thirty-six inches, and they don't get chewed up by bugs or mottled with disease. Give them a dose of 5-10-5, water and a benign smile. That's all they need. Zones 3-10.

Siberian Iris

Japanese iris

Japanese Iris: Another subsection that are great border plants. They are also known as *Kaempferi* or *Higo irises*. These beautiful plants grow from three to five feet on tall, sturdy stems, above foliage that is wider than the Siberian type. The flowers which show in July are huge, about nine inches in diameter. These orchid-like blossoms are ruffled and come in white, purple, lavender, pink, and royal blue. Try them in a collection, in the flower border or in a pocket by themselves. They can take shade and extremely moist soil, even the banks of a pond, provided the soil drains well. If you give them plenty of room, you don't have to divide them more than every five years or so. One precaution: they hate lime, so work in plenty of peat moss into the soil around them. Failure is most commonly caused by sweet soil; otherwise these are easy to grow. Zones 4-8.

Junipers: Lovely evergreens which are useful as a groundcover or in rock gardens. See chapters 9 or 7.

Lantana: A lovely patio plant that blooms all summer and can be wintered indoors in the North. See chapter 10.

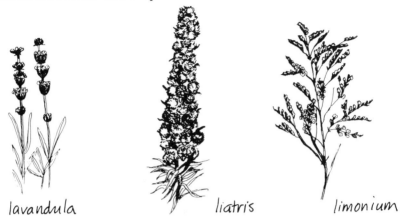

lavandula   liatris   limonium

Lavandula (lavender):   These are perennial herbs with fragrant blossoms and foliage. They grow to about eighteen inches, with silvery, needle-shaped leaves. The tiny pealike blooms cover the wiry stems in shades of violet and blue during most of July and August. A bunch of them in the front of the border in full sun needs only water and an annual feeding. There are dwarves which are pretty in the rock garden, also. Don't ever divide them, and don't ignore them either. Zones 5-10.

Liatris (gayfeather):   This border perennial blooms in spikes that grow from the dwarf, "Kobold" at eighteen inches, to tall background turrets of five feet. The flower spikes are one-and-a-half foot vertical wands with tiny, fuzzy blooms in white or purple. The taller varieties flower in late summer. The dwarf blooms from late July to September. They are lovely for drying and for accents in the flower bed and among shrubs. Sun or partial shade and a lot of moisture. Divide them every four years. Zones 2-8.

Lilium (hybrid lily):   A great border star. See chapter 10.

Limonium (sea lavender):   This is a great plant for the seashore, but even if you're landlocked, don't miss it. The stems are stiff and sturdy, and smothered with small purple or pink florets from late July to late August. They are easy to dry by just removing their water. They last well into the fall. Give them a dry, hot, sunny place in the front of the border. Don't divide them. Zones 3-10.

Iris cristata *and ferns bring color and foliage to a natural garden in the shade.*

Linum (flax):   This delightful perennial is one with a very long blooming season, starting in early June and frequently going until frost. Yellow flax shows a profusion of small blossoms on foliage that remains neat all season. Blue flax has dainty one-inch flowers with a creamy center. There is also an excellent white variety. They all grow to about eighteen inches. Give them sun, water, and never divide them. If a plant starts to get less energetic after four years or so, just replace it. They may not be long-lived, but they are pretty, reliable, and carefree. Zones 4-10.

Lychnis (catchfly or campion):   The *lychnis* is a plant with some very desirable traits for the low-care garden. The variety known as "Maltese Cross" is the *lychnis chalcedonia,* my favorite. It has lime green, bushy foliage which is capped by bright orange red clusters of florets in June and July. It grows to about two-three feet, in sun or part shade, and never needs dividing. Zones 3-9.

linum   lychnis   lythrum

Lythrum (purple loosestrife):   This is one of my favorite perennials. There is a purple *lythrum* that grows to only about twenty inches, as well as taller varieties that reach thirty-six inches. Sun or shade and plenty of moisture are their only requirements. The one-inch blossoms grow on tall spikes above willowy foliage. The flowers which show all summer long are bright pink or purple. A heavy rain sometimes topples a spike, but there are at least six or seven on each plant, so you won't miss it. Even when the stems droop in heavy rain, they regain their erect posture a short while later. They are great for naturalizing, but in the border, divide them every four years or so. Zones 3-9.

Monarda (bee balm or bergamot):   All *monarda* have fragrant, mintlike foliage. They grow to about two-and-a-half feet in a sunny spot or in shade. They love moisture but make no other demands. The lower leaves sometimes get discolored, but this is harmless to the plant. The flowers, which are exotic-looking whorls of thin petals, appear in mid-July for about one month. Just before blooming, the top leaves around the bud turn dark pink or scarlet. Flowers come in white, pink, red, and a striking blue. Divide them every four years, and watch out for the bees they attract. Zones 3-8.

monarda   nepeta   oenothera

Myrica Pensylvanica (bayberry):   An excellent shrub for the seashore. See chapter 12.

Nepeta (catmint):   There are two varieties of *nepeta* named *mussinii* and *fassenii,* and different catalogues make extravagant claims about each. I have found that they are both delightful, but the *fassenii* blooms for a longer period. It blooms from early June to mid-August, with hundreds of tiny flowers on crinkly, gray green foliage. The florets are a bright purple, and they look delightful in the front of the border or in the rock garden, since they grow only about fifteen inches tall. *Nepeta* never needs dividing, and the little sprays of flowers, when grown tightly together, look charming with other bright yellow flowers. They prefer bright, hot sun, but tolerate periods of drought. Zones 3-10.

Oenothera (evening sundrops or evening primrose):   The stiff, long, and elegant leaves of this low-growing perennial create compact mounds topped by large yellow flowers. The seed pods are about two inches long and dark brown. This hardy plant grows to about eighteen inches and blooms all summer. It likes dry soil in sun or very light shade. Although it is very carefree, bugs will attack the leaves, so spray carefully. This plant is best in the rock garden or in the front of the border. Not great, but never needs dividing and is reliable. Zones 4-10.

Pachysandra (spurge):   The best groundcover of all. See chapter 9.

Pentstemon (beard tongue):   This perennial grows in leafy mounds which throw tall spires with a profusion of tubular flowers in pretty shades of blue, lavender, red, or orange. There is a lovely dwarf, "Newberry" which grows to one foot and flowers in June. Two other hybrids are excellent and bloom from June to September. One is the thirty-six-inch tall "Prairie Fire," and the other bright pink "Rose Elf," reaches only eighteen inches. They all need sun or light shade, good drainage, and some protection in winter. They are easy to care for and need dividing every three years. Plant and divide only in the spring. Zones 5-10.

Peony: One of the star perennials. See chapter 10.

Philadelphus (mock orange): A lovely shrub, small enough to be part of the perennial border. See chapter 13.

Phlox: The moss *phlox* is the star of the rock garden. See chapter 7. The tall, border *phlox* is the star of the perennial border. See chapter 10. Use them both.

penstemon   platycodon

Platycodon (balloon flower): The starlike flowers of this great perennial open from swollen buds which appear like balloons. Guess where its common name came from. The foliage is a bright, leathery green, and bushy. It grows to about two feet, and the bell-like flowers come in blue, white, or shell pink. They grow in sun or shade, any kind of soil, and alongside any neighbors. The only thing they hate is transplanting or moving, so leave them alone. Insects never find them, and disease stays away even in an infested border. If this sounds like a hard pitch, it is. Buy them and enjoy their flowers in July and August. Zones 3-10.

Polygonum (fleeceflower): Excellent groundcover. See chapter 9.

Potentilla (shrubby cinquefoil): Wonderful shrubs for the perennial border or for hedges. See chapter 13.

Primula (primrose): In early spring, a shady section of the rock garden, or the front of a border, or a pocket planting in a shady, moist corner is immeasurably brightened by these easy-to-like and easy-to-grow perennials. There are dozens of hardy species in every color of the rainbow, and a variety of shapes including low, small clusters, or tall, flowering stems with blossoms about an inch wide. They all grow out of a rosette of foliage with stems from six inches to two feet. The easiest to grow are the *polyanthas* or the *japonicas,* which flower until mid-June. Divide them every other year, after they flower. The clumps are shallow rooted and easily fall into divisions by themselves. They look best in a mass, and they are eager to grow and spread in shady, moist beds. Zones 4-10.

Rosa Rugosa: Rose shrubs, good for the seashore. See chapter 12.

Salvia (perennial sage): If you study the blooming periods of the varieties of this perennial, you can have lovely lavender and blue flowers from May until frost, with only a few plants. They all have excellent foliage which displays florets on sturdy stems, rising from eight to forty inches, depending on the hybrid. Sun and water are all they need. Don't divide them. The longest blooming *salvia* is "Haematodes" which flowers from June to September on thirty-six-inch stems. The "May Night" *salvia* grows to about twenty inches and has bright violet flowers from May into August. All *salvias* are lovely and dependable. Zones 3-10.

Saponaria: A great plant for wall gardens. See chapter 7.

primula

salvia

Daylilies and astilbe *are both lovely in this naturalized garden.*

Sedum and Sempervivum: *Sedum,* known as stonecrop, comes in so many varieties that it is impossible to classify them here. Most of them have fleshy leaves in small whorls or needlelike growth. Flowers vary. Some are bright pink or red sprays, and others appear like tiny, yellow stars. Many are rampant and will cover a boulder in a few months. Use them in difficult, dry areas, but always keep the fast spreaders away from the perennial flower border or they'll become a pest. The *sempervivum,* known as hens and chicks, look like rosettes which proliferate by forming new flowers at their bases. Look for the ones with pretty pink edges. They are great for wall gardens. See chapter 7.

Sidalcea (false mallow):   Here's a pretty pink flower that resembles hollyhocks, but it doesn't need staking, and it lives longer. *Sidalcea* grows to about three feet and shows pink blossoms on sturdy spikes. The foliage is scalloped, and lobed, and attractive all season. A hybrid named "Rosy Gem" is just that, and it flowers in July and August. Only sun, and water, and division every four years or so. Zones 5-10.

Thalictrum (meadow rue):   There is only one hybrid of this perennial that is outstanding for the border. It is the *rochebrunianum,* known as the lavender mist meadow rue. It has fernlike foliage similar to *aquilegia,* grows to about three feet in sun or shade, and showers lovely, dancing, lavender blossoms with yellow centers, about an inch wide, from mid-July to fall. It never needs dividing. You may also want to see the dusty meadow rue with fuzzy sprays of yellow flowers. Look for nurseries that offer these easy-care perennials. Zones 5-10.

sidalcea   thalictrum   Carolina thermopsis

Thermopsis (Carolinian lupine): This low-maintenance perennial has flowers that resemble the lupines. Small pealike florets grow along ten-inch spikes above pretty foliage. This plant grows to about three feet in sun or light shade. The bright yellow flower spikes look lovely in the back of the border, and they show all of June and July. After bloom you can cut some of the foliage down. It never needs dividing and should be more popular than it is. Zones 3-10.

Hybrid lilium *looks like an aristocrat but is a low-maintenance, rewarding perennial worthy of room in any garden.*

Thyme: Herb that makes a lovely rock garden plant. Chapter 7.

Tradescantia (spiderwort):   There's another ugly common name for such pretty and dependable flowers. Although they grow in the sun, shade brings out their best performance. They have violet-shaped flowers in white, pink, red, purple, or blue. The foliage is grasslike, and the new varieties stay upright and display their flowers all summer. If you give them room to spread in a natural garden, they won't need dividing, but in the border, they should be separated every four years or so. Most of them grow from eighteen inches to two-and-a-half feet. Zones 4-10.

Trillium (trout lily):   Pretty wildflower. See chapter 12.

Trollius (globeflower):   The flowers of this perennial are sunny yellow or orange. They are buttercuplike and grow from deeply cut, bright green foliage. In a moist, shady area they grow to about two-and-a-half feet. They bloom in May and June, but if cut back, may grow a second or even third batch of flowers. They are very pretty and easy to grow, and need dividing only every four years or so. I don't divide mine, and after five years they still flower prolifically. Zones 3-10.

Tunica (tunic flower):   Lovely rock garden plant. See chapter 7.

Valerian (garden heliotrope):   This excellent border perennial is also classified as *centranthus*. Whatever it's called, it is very valuable in the border. The foliage is bright green and very leafy. The flowers are terminal sprays of thousands of tiny florets in bright pink or white. The stems reach about two-and-a-half feet and flower from June until frost. Insects and disease seem to miss it. The white does not spread as quickly as the pink variety, but both colors are lovely. Sun or shade, good soil, and plenty of moisture are all *valerian* needs. It's supposedly fragrant, but I don't smell anything perfumy about it. I do prize *valerian*, though. It blooms continuously, and requires so little care. Spring planting only. Dividing not necessary. Zones 3-10.

tradescantia

trollius

Veronica (speedwell):   This excellent perennial has varieties that bloom from early spring to mid-July, from early August to frost, and those like "Crater Lake Blue" and "Barcarole" which bloom all summer long. They are all lovely, including the little dwarves for the rock garden and the tall blue and white hybrids that grow to two-and-a-half feet. "Barcarole" grows to only about ten inches with pink flowers, and "Crater Lake Blue" grows to about two feet. They all have dark green foliage with firm oval leaves, and the flowers are spikes or turrets on stiff stems. They like sun or light shade, ordinary soil, and a permanent place in the garden. Never move or divide them. Try them all. Zones 4-10.

Vinca (periwinkle):   Lovely groundcover for shade or sun. See chapter 9.

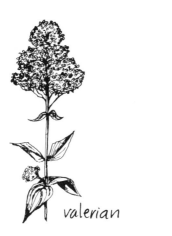

valerian

veronica

RECOMMENDED BOOKS

Crockett, James U. *Perennials.* Alexandria, Virginia: Time-Life Books.

Hay, Roy, and Synge, Patrick M. *Color Dictionary of Flowers and Plants for Home and Garden.* New York: Crown Publishers, Inc.

Hebb, Robert S. *Low Maintenance Perennials.* New York: Quadrangle/The New York Times Book Co., Inc.

Pierot, Suzanne Warner. *What Can I Grow in the Shade?* New York: Liveright.

Van Pelt Wilson, Helen. *Successful Gardening With Perennials.* New York: Doubleday & Co., Inc.

Wallach, Carla. *The Reluctant Weekend Gardener.* New York: Macmillan, Inc.

Wyman, Donald. *Wyman's Gardening Encyclopedia.* New York: Macmillan, Inc.

CATALOGUES

Wayside Gardens Catalogue. Hodges, South Carolina.

White Flower Farm Catalogue. Litchfield, Connecticut.

index